DEATH
ON THE
WATERWAYS

POLICE · BUDGET · EDITION

EDITED BY HAROLD FURNISS

FAMOUS CRIMES

PAST AND PRESENT

ONE · PENNY

DEATH
ON THE
WATERWAYS

ALLAN SCOTT-DAVIES

Frontispiece: Burke and Hare used their friends to get their victims drunk before they murdered them. (*Famous Crimes*)

First published 2011

The History Press
The Mill, Brimscombe Port
Stroud, Gloucestershire, GL5 2QG
www.thehistorypress.co.uk

British Library Cataloguing in Publication Data.
A catalogue record for this book is available from the British Library.

ISBN 978 0 7524 5966 0

Typesetting and origination by The History Press
Printed in in the EU for The History Press.

CONTENTS

INTRODUCTION

The tragic ways that the victims contained within these pages met their ends include canals and rivers, quarries and pools and even the seemingly innocent bath tub. There are grizzly tales of premeditated murders, and of murders motivated out of love, hate and jealousy. The research for this book has not been easy as the work has taken me deep into the darker side of life – and death. Every murder has a victim with a past of their own that, given today's modern internet access and the many books out there on the subject, can be followed in as much detail as one wishes. The people involved in the deaths become 'real' to us as their story is written, as with the murder of young Olive Turner who was taken from her family and a new flourishing love by a wicked, unhinged man who lived in a world where he believed he could harm without retribution. And this has been the dilemma: to cover these murders in a way that is not dramatic or theatrical and yet get across the terror, sadness and pain; and to preserve respect for the victim, and sometimes for the murderer too, for example in the cases of some of the women executed for infanticide. There were fathers who took the lives of their wives and sometimes children too, as the pressures of life took over; one man acted with such sudden rage that he murdered his newborn children as they were suckling on their mother, having already drowned his three others. The list goes on and includes the Victorian trade of baby farming, eventually stamped out through the Infant Life Protection Act of 1897 and the Children's Act of 1908, and the likes of Amelia Dyer who murdered 400 innocent children for money. Accidents also happened in the excavation of tunnels for the many canals that collapsed, taking the lives of those working deep inside the earth. The navvies suffered working on the reservoirs, cuttings for the canals and in the industrial age of engineering developments, when many were blown up, crushed, smashed or simply died of overwork and undernourishment.

Waterways have always been a part of life across the UK. Early accounts of murder and mayhem include the raids carried out by the Danish invaders of Saxon England. They were said to have sailed up the River Severn to raid Worcester and even Bridgnorth in Shropshire, where they killed and took hostage many people. That was in 894. It is true on a spring tide the River Severn has the natural phenomenon called the Severn bore, which means that the Danes perhaps did get as far as Worcester, but it is highly improbable that they made it to Bridgnorth, as it has been recorded.

In the Middle Ages the rivers were used to transport cargo, yet this was a slow and laborious way of moving goods. However, the River Thames had become London's highway, taking goods far up the river from the port area around the East End. The Thames is a short length compared to the River Severn in the fourteenth century, which was deep and fast flowing, making it was possible to get a vessel from Bristol to Bewdley and then by smaller boats upstream as far as Shrewsbury in Shropshire. By the seventeenth century the upper limit was extended to Welshpool in Powys. The keeping open of this river was partly due to the great tides that flushed through the Bristol Channel, thus keeping the estuary clear. It also became known as the King's High Stream, or King's Water Highway, as the Severn was a free river throughout the full navigable length. Unfortunately other rivers were hampered by heavy river tolls based on the type of goods carried, which pushed a lot of goods off the waterways and on to carts, as happened to the canals in the late 1940s and 1950s.

An interesting case of inland piracy occurred in the reign of Henry VI when Tewkesbury had trouble with the Forest of Dean men who, with a great rise in numbers and a manner of war, acted as enemies of the king. Marauding along the Welsh banks of the River Severn, they captured vessels to steal the cargo, murder their crews if they had not jumped into the river first, and sink the boats. The complaint to the king about the trouble was eventually settled by an Act of Parliament in 1430. This declared that because the River Severn was used to carry all his people to Bristol, Gloucester and Worcester, as well as all manner of merchandise, trows and boats, which many Welshmen and others had taken to dragging to pieces and beating the men in them for a ransom, all such persons so offended should be preceded against accordingly in the course of the common law. This basically meant that anyone attacking the boats on the King's Water Highway could be taken and hung, drawn and quartered.

During the Industrial Revolution the river was used to transport goods from the Coalbrookdale works in Shropshire down to Bristol and out to the rest of the world. There were a number of Acts passed to allow people to use the rivers to transport goods: the River Witham, Trent and the Yorkshire Ouse and portions of the Swale, Ure, Wharfe and Derwent. Each Act, however, gave rise to even more crime. There were a lot of disputes along the routes where owners and tenants of land suddenly found great gangs of hauliers stomping over their land, breaking down fences, even taking the livestock at will. In 1540 Henry VIII passed an Act regulating tolls upon the rivers, which was still in force in 1820. This provided a scale of how much people should be charged for using the waterways, and thus a tax to keep the waterways navigable.

As time moved on a number of rivers were canalised – their banks were straightened with towpaths placed on the left- or right-side bank to aid boat travel. In eastern England a large number of rivers, the Witham, Welland, Glen, Nene and Great Ouse, were used to help the drainage of the fens, but also allowed straight navigable rivers to be designed and built. The River Lark in the east was made navigable from Mildenhall Mill to Bury St Edmunds in Suffolk. As the first throes of the industrial revolution started to take grip on the need for better transportation of goods, Francis Edgerton, third Duke of Bridgewater, passed an Act that led to making a navigable cut or canal from a certain place in the township of Salford to, or as near as possible to, Worsley Mill and Middlewood, in the manner of Worsley to Hollin Ferry in Lancashire. He teamed up with one of the country's best-known canal builders, James Brindley, who was born in 1716. Although self-taught, Brindley was a natural genius and is said to have been the forerunner of both civil and mechanical engineering. Bridgewater and Brindley were joined by Earl Gower and they started work on the first canal from Worsley to Manchester. On a scale of later canal projects it was a minor one at just 10½ miles long, but when it opened in July 1761 and the first boatload of coal sailed across the aqueduct, known as the castle in the air, it was called a marvel. To get around, over and through the terrain, Brindley devised weirs, culverts, stop gates and other canal-related construction ideas that we can see today. In those early days Brindley went on to design and build over 260 miles of canals.

The birth of the Fradely junction to the Thames and the Birmingham to Fazeley Canal led to a sudden rush of navvies to these areas of often quiet countryside. And this was the problem. Once the canal line had been agreed with landowners, unlike today there were no JCBs or earth-moving equipment, just many hundreds of hardworking navvies. Not only were there the navvies, there were also the ladies of the camp who came with them, and often a brewer, a baker and a shopkeeper. They were all employed by the same people and were issued with company money or tokens. For the employer and owner it was a wonderful situation to be in as they could charge what they wanted, particularly when the navvies were miles from any town or village pub. A tented village grew up around the cut, leaving trails of litter and destruction behind as the construction moved along the route. Fights often broke out between the navvies and the locals, thefts were commonplace and occasionally there was a murder – perhaps a local catching a navvy in the act of stealing chickens and having his or her throat cut, or navvies caught by locals who then beat them up, often leaving them for dead either in the workings or the already flooded canal.

As you will see throughout this book, waterways have seen much violence and precipitated many accidents from early history to the present. There are still raised fists when a narrowboat dares disturb someone fishing along the towpath or riverbank and there have been sudden deaths in locks, slow carbon monoxide poisoning in sealed boats and vandalism that can, and often does, lead to injury and death. Quarries and lime pits have their own grim place in this book as locations where bodies can easily be hidden or where workers have been crushed, blown up or drowned in the many waterfilled pits and shafts abundant in such places. As in the past, theft, violence, vandalism and murder still occur along our waterways, yet they are also some of the most peaceful and beautiful places to work, travel or just stand and watch life pass by.

1

Disasters

 Disasters on the waterways often involve large numbers of victims, be they on board a ship or train or just watching an event, such as the accident on the River Lea. The famous shipbuilders Thames Ironworks was to lead the way ship launches would be organised following an accident during the launch of HMS *Albion*. On 21 June 1898 nearly 30,000 people had crammed into the shipyard to watch the launch presided over by the Duchess of York. It was such a community event that the schools and yard workers were given the day off. The excitement was great and some 200 spectators had made their way onto a temporary wooden bridge structure on the opposite side of the river at Bow Creek, which is a narrow yet very deep part of the river. The near-completed *Shikishima* for the Japanese navy, which rested between the bridge and the *Albion*, partly obscured the view from the riverbank, causing a rush of spectators to the wooden structure. The police and yard workers tried to clear the bridge several times but failed to keep people off when the *Albion* was launched after three failed attempts to smash the bottle of champagne against her hull. As she entered the river the *Albion* sent a huge wave of water into the bridge, smashing it to pieces and throwing people into the river and to their deaths. Their screams were not heard over the clapping and cheering following the launch of the ship. Unaware of any problems, the duke, duchess and the crowds started to move away from the podium with thoughts of the afternoon tea that had been laid on by the company. It was a good ten minutes before news of the accident came through to the site managers and the main bulk of the crowd, although spectators and workers nearby had begun immediate rescue efforts. Spectators jumped into the muddy waters to help survivors. The Thames police used a rowing boat to rescue people and the Ironworks Ambulance Corps were soon on the scene doing their best to save those in the water and remove the bodies of the thirty-eight people, including women and children, who died instantly.

The chairman of the works, Arnold Hills, was so devastated by the disaster that he promised to meet all funeral expenses and contributed to a fund set up by West Ham Council to help the survivors. Many of the dead were among the poorest in London, with a high number of those who died being the sole wage earners for the family. On the route to East London cemetery the week after the accident, huge crowds gathered to catch sight of the funeral procession and pay their respects. The oldest victim at sixty-four was Mrs Eliza Tarbot and she was the first to be buried, followed by Mrs Isobel White, thirty, and her two children Lottie, five, and Queenie, two. When Mrs White was pulled out of the water her daughters were still clinging to her frock and they were all drowned. There is a memorial to the victims of the *Albion* disaster in East London cemetery in the form of an anchor on a stone base. The *Albion* went on to serve in the Middle East during the First World War and was eventually sold off as scrap in December 1918 – a short life for a very proud ship.

Albion disaster shipyard. (Thames Ironworks)

The late nineteenth century saw the River Thames becoming increasingly busy. There were hundreds of vessels ranging from large liners to tugs, barges and lighters sailing up and down the river, yet there were no clear instructions about how the river should be navigated. In 1878 this all changed when the paddle steamer *Princess Alice*, captained by William Grinstead, sank after a collision in Gallions Reach, close to Woolwich town. With over 600 people on board, including the captain and his family, most of these passengers were to lose their lives in what is still the worst disaster to occur on British waterways. *Princess Alice* was launched at Rennick in 1865 and some say that when her name was changed from *Bute* things started to go wrong, as it is believed in seagoing traditions that to change a name of a ship is bad luck. She served a year sailing from Wemyss to the Isle of Arran for the Wemyss Railway Company and in 1866 she was bought by the Watermans Steam Packet Company, who renamed her *Princess Alice*, serving as a Thames excursion boat for twelve years.

On 3 September 1878 she made a routine trip from Swan pier, near London Bridge, to Gravesend and Sheerness carrying hundreds of Londoners who had visited Rosherville Gardens in Gravesend. She left Gravesend at 6p.m. and just before 8p.m. that evening she had completed most of her return journey, passing Tripcock Point, and entered the part of the river known as Gallions Reach. The *Princess Alice* was a matter of minutes from the North Woolwich pier, where many of the passengers were to leave the vessel. At the same time the *Bywell Castle* was steaming towards her. She was a larger vessel, being a steam collier at 890 tons. The *Bywell Castle* had just been repainted and was returning down the Thames from Millwall docks towards Newcastle to pick up cargo destined for Egypt.

As there were no rules about how vessels were to pass each other, as well as unreliable currents and strong tides, vessels navigated the river according to the experience of the captain. Captain Harris was on the bridge of the *Bywell Castle* when he noticed the *Princess Alice* as she cut across his bow line from the north side of the river. Altering his course, he intended to pass safely astern of her but at that point the captain of the *Princess Alice* suddenly changed direction, bringing the paddle steamer into the path of the oncoming collier. When the ships were about 400 yards apart Captain Harris ordered stokers in the engine room to reverse the engines of the *Bywell Castle*, but it was too late. The collier struck the *Princess Alice* near her stern paddle wheel and, unable to survive such a blow, the paddle steamer split into two and sank within four minutes.

Recovering bodies from the River Thames following the *Princess Alice* disaster.

The light at this point was fading fast. Very few of the passengers died from the collision; most either drowned inside the ship or trying to escape the clinging waters of the River Thames. At the time, this scenario was made drastically worse by the filthy Thames water which contained raw sewage and heavy pollutants that flowed straight into the river from industrial plants at North Greenwich and Silverton. Moreover there was little in the way of directional help other than gas lights from the shore. The survivors of the collision struggled to reach safety. Many of the women had little chance of survival as they rarely knew how to swim and their clothing, once wet, would become terribly heavy, dragging them down under the cold Thames water. The crew of the *Bywell Castle* threw down ropes, launched boats and picked up a handful of survivors. The loud explosion and noisy creaking and groaning of the ship before she went down attracted many people to look across at the accident from the banks. The manager of the Becton Gasworks sent out boats which returned with just twenty-five people; in all just 100 people survived.

As the news of the disaster spread crowds gathered on the North Woolwich pier and at the London Steamboat Company's offices in the city. A company spokesman read out the names of the survivors to those who waited anxiously for news of their families and friends. But it soon became obvious that very few passengers had survived the accident. News soon reached captains of other vessels on the river who began to see bodies floating down the river towards them. One man described it as seeing a sea of men, women and children floating towards him and he and his crew pulled the bodies out hoping that some of them would be survivors. Over ninety bodies were recovered from the river in the first week of the collision and others up to three months later as the river gave them up, bloated with gas and some partly eaten by rats. Bodies were also recovered from the two halves of the *Princess Alice* when she was raised from the bed of the Thames. After much lifting the two halves of the ship were eventually grounded. When the police went in they found many bodies, including those of children, crushed together against locked exit doors on the lower decks. Many of the bodies had been in the polluted water so long that it was impossible to make a formal identification; to this day they remain unknown, with 120 of them buried as unidentified. It is believed that around 640 people lost their lives in the tragedy. There were stories of survival aided by air pockets in some women's dresses that had ballooned when they were thrown into the river, helping them keep afloat until rescue, and one gentleman stood on the bow of the boat and simply stepped on to a rescue boat as the *Princess Alice* sank beneath him. One family lost three generations to the disaster. William Towse, the manager of the steamship company, had taken his four sons, wife and parents on a treat to see the Rosherville Gardens for afternoon tea; not one member of the family survived. The bodies were landed at Woolwich, where a church hall and sheds of local companies were taken over as temporary mortuaries. A diver who went to the ship before she was landed to be searched found she had broken into three pieces: bow, engine and stern sections. At low tide that morning police caught two local criminals searching the bodies for cash and charged the two offenders, placing a watch on the wreck. A memorial was erected following public subscription in Woolwich churchyard.

The inquest into the collision took place at Woolwich Town Hall where the coroner and expert witnesses tried to establish what happened on that fateful day. For the next ten weeks more than 100 witnesses were called, including survivors, who gave their account of the disaster. Eventually the jury returned a verdict of death by misadventure, making the collision an accident. There were criticisms of both captains, with some saying the captain of the collier should have stopped engines earlier and the paddle steamer captain should have stopped when he saw the collier bearing down on him. The shipping company who owned the fated *Princess Alice* was also criticised for having too many passengers on board a ship that was only meant to carry 400 and the fact that there were few lifeboats and the few there were had been padlocked to the ship. The board of trade conducted its own hearing and they concluded that both captains had shown poor judgement. They recommended that two vessels under steam should pass each other on the port side.

In 1880 new rules for navigating the Thames came into force that would tighten up procedures for steamships passing on the river to reduce the number of passengers they could carry and increase the number of easily accessible lifebelts that vessels had to provide. In the early 1880s the Thames division of the Metropolitan Police were provided with steam launches to replace row boats.

The captain of the *Princess Alice*, his wife and two sons were amongst those who perished on that September evening. The captain of *Bywell Castle* continued at the helm; however, in 1883 she was listed on the Lloyd's Register as missing in the Bay of Biscay with all hands lost. The wreck of the *Princess Alice* was quickly scrapped, yet a number of mementos from her were turned into souvenirs of the great disaster and were sold to tourists close to where she sank.

A journalist, W. T. Vincent, on the scene very early on wrote:

Soon policeman and watermen were seen by the feeble light bearing ghastly objects into the offices of the steamboat company, for a boat has just arrived with the first consignment of the dead, mostly little children whose light body and ample drapery had kept them afloat even while they were smothered in the festering Thames. I followed into the steamboat office, marvelling at the fate which had brought the earliest harvest of victims to the headquarters of the doomed ship, and, entering the boardroom, the first of the martyrs was pointed out to me as one of the companies own servants, a man employed on the Princess Alice, brought here thus soon to attest by his silent presence the ship's identity. The lifeless frames of men and women lay about, and out on the balcony, from which the directors had too often looked upon their fleet through the fragrant smell of evening cigar, there was a sight to ring out tears of blood from the eyes of any beholder. A row of little innocents, plump and pretty, well-dressed children, all dead and cold, some with life's ruddy tinge still in their cheeks and lips, the lips from which the merry prattle had gone for ever. Callous as one may grow from frequent contact with terrors and afflictions, one could never be inured to this. It was a spectacle to move the most hardened official and dwell forever in his dreams. Then to think what was beyond out there in the river. It was madness.

Another notable disaster happened on the first bridge over the River Tay, built to the designs of Sir Thomas Bouch, which took six years to build, used over 10 million bricks, 2 million rivets, 87,000 cubic feet of timber and 15,000 barrels of cement. All the materials were put together by 600 men, twenty of whom were either crushed to death or fell into the river below and drowned. They worked in shifts around the clock in all conditions with little or no protective equipment. The bridge was opened on 26 September 1877 with all the pomp that could be mustered by the railway company. An invited group of dignitaries and directors of the company, joined by Sir Thomas, travelled in both directions where they admired the bridge and the never before seen views of the river. During a violent storm on the night of 28 December 1879, the middle section of the bridge collapsed taking with it a passenger train and all seventy-five passengers. The son-in-law of the designer was one of the victims of the disaster, which was caused by high winds that the construction design of the bridge had not allowed for.

The Times, on 29 December 1879, reported from Dundee at midnight:

Loss of the passenger train.
Tonight a heavy gale swept over Dundee and a portion of the Tay Bridge was blown down while the train from Edinburgh due at 7.15 was passing. It is believed that the train is in the water, but the gale is still so strong the steamboat has not yet been able to reach the bridge. The train was duly signalled from Fife as having entered the bridge at 7.14. It was seen running along the rails, and then suddenly was observed a flash of fire. Opinion was that the train left the rails, and went over the bridge. Those who saw the incident repaired immediately to the Tay Bridge station at Dundee and informed the station master of what they had seen. He immediately put himself in communication with the men in charge of the signal box at the North end of the bridge. The telegraph wires were stretched across the bridge, when the instrument was tried it was soon seen the wires were broken.

Searching for the passengers and train. (*Christian Herald*)

Tay Bridge disaster, showing fallen middle section. (*Christian Herald*)

Mr Smith, the station master and Mr Roberts, locomotive super-intendent, determined, notwithstanding the fierce gale, to walk across the bridge as far as possible from the North side, to view of ascertaining the extent of the disaster. They were able to get out a considerable distance, and the first thing that caught their eye was the water spurting from a pipe which was laid across the bridge for the supply of Newport, a village on the south side, from Dundee reservoirs. Going a little further, they could distinctly see by the aid of a strong moonlight that there was a large gap in the bridge caused by the fall, so far as they could discern, of two or three of the largest spars. They thought, however, that they observed a red light on the south part of the bridge, and were of the opinion that the train had been brought to a standstill on the driver noticing the accident. This conjecture was, unfortunately, to be proved incorrect. At Broughtyferry, four miles from the bridge, several mailbags have come ashore, and there is no doubt that the train is in the river. No precise information as to the number of passengers can be obtained, but it is variously estimated at from 150 to 200.

The train engine was recovered from the river. (*Christian Herald*)

The broken central section of the bridge. (*Christian Herald*)

Front page report of
the Tay Bridge disaster.
(*Christian Herald*)

The provost and a number of leading citizens of Dundee started at half past
10 o'clock in the steamboat for the bridge, the gale being moderated; but
they have not yet returned.

Monday, 1.30a.m. – (*The Times* report)
The scene at Tay Bridge Station tonight is simply appalling. Many thousand
persons are congregated around the buildings, and strong men or women
are wringing their hands in despair. On the 2nd of October 1877, while the
bridge was in course of construction, one of the girders was blown down
during a gale similar to that of today, but the only one of the workmen lost
his life. The return of the steamboat is anxiously waited.

At the inquiry that followed engineers found that the columns supporting
the thirteen longest spans were weak, leading to the collapse. The design had

Illustrated report of the disaster. (*Christian Herald*)

not allowed for the stress of gales despite the fact that a section of the bridge collapsed in a gale whilst under construction, when one man was killed as he fell with the truss into the river. So great was his distress at the loss of so many lives, Sir Thomas passed away in his sleep less than a year later. There is a famous poem by William Topaz McGonagall about the disaster, part of which is given below:

The Tay Bridge Disaster

Beautiful Railway Bridge of the Silv'ry Tay!
Alas! I am very sorry to say
That ninety lives have been taken away
On the last Sabbath day of 1879,
Which will be remember'd for a very long time.

So the train mov'd slowly along the Bridge of Tay,
Until it was about midway,
Then the central girders with a crash gaveway,
And down went the train and passengers into the Tay,
The storm fiend did loudly bray,
Because ninety lives have been taken away,
On the last Sabbath day of 1879,
Which will be remember'd for a very long time.

As soon as the catastrophe came to be known
The alarm from mouth to mouth was blown,
And the cry rang out all o'er the town,
Good Heavens! the Tay Bridge is blown down,
And a passenger train from Edinburgh,
Which fill'd all the people's hearts with sorrow,
And made them for water turned pale,
Because none of the passengers were sav'd to tell the tale
How the disaster happen'd on the last Sabbath day of 1879,
Which will be remember'd for a very long time.

Another disaster that resulted in loss of life came to be known as the Blow-up Bridge Disaster. The Macclesfield Bridge crosses the Regent's Canal in the north-west corner of London's Regent's Park. The original bridge was built very solidly with three brick arches supported in the centre by two rows of sturdy cast-iron columns, made in Coalbrookdale, Shropshire. On top it had attractive iron railings on either side of a very handsome structure that was named after the Earl of Macclesfield, chairman of the canal company. Competition with the train for transporting goods was increasing yet it was still felt that the slower-paced canal boat was the best way of transporting explosives. It was considered that the presence of a high-pressure boiler and open firebox complemented by a chimney often shooting out hot flecks of ash and soot was not ideal for the transportation of explosives by train.

On Friday 2 October 1874, the narrowboat *Tilbury* was carrying a cargo of mixed goods, three barrels of petroleum and 5 tons of gunpowder made at Waltham Abbey Powder Mills and was bound for Codnor Park, near Nottingham. *Tilbury* was one of seven boats that had left London City Road basin at about three o'clock in the morning, towed by the steamer, *Ready*, heading towards their destination. Behind *Ready* was the fly boat

Tay Bridge

SUNDAY, DEC. 28, 1879

Oh ! Bonnie Dundee, Oh ! Bonnie Dundee,
Thy sorrow is ours, and our hearts bleed for thee,
As thou standest all speechless and stricken in woe,
Where thy river runs mad in its turbulent flow.

Oh ! Bonnie Dundee, to our childhood's glad ears,
The pibroch has sounded and chased all our fears,
And in manhood we hearken in joyance again,
As our feet beat the time to thy heart-stirring strain.

But now when we listen to " Bonnie Dundee,"
'Tis the crowd, and the wringing of hands we shall see,
And thy bridge o'er the Tay, like a beautiful chain,
With the links rudely sunder'd, to meet ne'er again.

'Tis the moan in the distance, the sigh in the wind,
That will wake a sad chord as it brings thee to mind;
The gap in the moonlight ! the dark gulf below !
And the terrible anguish that no man will know !

Oh ! brave men who tremble, and strong ones who fail,
If England's deep sympathy will not avail,
There is solace for hearts that are broken and riven,
Not in those deep waters—but upward in Heaven.

A. GASKELL

named *Jane* carrying a small quantity of gunpowder, followed by *Dee*, then *Tilbury, Limehouse* and *Hawkesbury*. Just before five o'clock in the morning *Tilbury* was under the Macclesfield Bridge when the gunpowder on the boat ignited and an enormous explosion occurred. The boat was blown to pieces, all those on board were killed and a huge crater was left behind. Early reports indicated there were four fatalities: Baxton, thirty-five, William Taylor, a labourer aged twenty-five, another man and a boy, their names unknown. Records were often kept on the boat and sometimes steerers, as they were called, would help the boatmen make sure the boat they were on stayed in line and were often casual day workers.

The damage was extensive. The barge behind was sunk and the bridge completely demolished, with bricks and debris thrown in all directions and heavy cast-iron columns thrown around like ninepins. The park's superintendent's house nearby was completely wrecked and there was a great deal of damage to glass in the zoological society gardens close by. Nearby houses also suffered extensive damage to windows, walls and furniture. The roof in one house 300 yards away suffer badly when part of the *Tilbury's* keel fell on its roof and went right through to the basement, yet miraculously no one was killed or injured in the house. Chaos was also caused by fracturing of gas and water mains carried on the bridge and telegraph wires were severed, which hampered communication during rescue work.

Such was the explosion that many residents woke from their slumbers and rushed into the streets in panic wondering if the end of the world had come. The police and fire services arrived as soon as they could but needed the help of the Horse Guards from Albany to calm the crowd down; by this timr many were screaming and running about in confusion. Dr William Collins, who lived nearby on Primrose Hill, hastened to the scene and assisted with the rescue efforts and administered first aid to many of the survivors. He also took photographs of the disaster later that day. Dr Collins gave evidence afterwards:

> ...a loud and deafening report with which fearfully shook the very foundations of the premises and a tremendous crash from the breaking of the plate and glass. On the streets I witnessed an extraordinary scene of men, women and children rushing about in a state of semi-nudity and that in the most horrendous cries wept about the streets. One lady in her nightdress clung to me exclaiming is it come, is it come.

Dr Collins went on to say in his notice that they had been enveloped in a dense, suffocating smoke that made them fear for their very lives.

The inquest into the deaths of those on the *Tilbury* recorded dangerous cargo on board and duly noted that there was also an open fire in the cabin and a lamp that was uncovered. It was only realised later how lucky everyone had been given the force of the explosion. Many newspapers carried the story very quickly and the *London Illustrated News* pointed out on 10 October that had the explosion occurred half an hour earlier or later or in the tunnel under Islington the damage would have been much worse. The fact that the explosion happened within a cutting under a very substantial bridge which took the brunt of the blast saved many lives. Furthermore the explosion was funnelled up and down the canal causing slight damage elsewhere.

Newspapers at the time were very forceful about their comments concerning the risk to the public resulting from the transportation of explosives. There was already a Gunpowder Act of 1860, although its provisions were inadequate and had not been properly observed, leaving the carriage of gunpowder, nitro-glycerine and substances of a similar kind virtually unregulated. The newspapers asked the Government to take prompt action to introduce proper safety controls; as a result of this, the Explosives Act 1875 was passed in order to introduce essential safeguards.

When the bridge came to be rebuilt it was found that all of the iron columns had survived the explosion so they were reused, a form of Victorian recycling. Today the bridge columns bear the rope marks on the inside that would have been on the outside the columns.

The inquest held at the Marylebone workhouse finally took place with a vital witness, William White of the *Dee*. White had been in hospital, too ill to attend any of the earlier inquiries, and eventually with his help a verdict was reached on 19 October 1874. Within five days of the tragedy the canal had been cleared and the exact number of people killed known. The hundreds that were reported in a newspaper turned out to be just three unlucky people, Charles Baxton, William Taylor, and Jonathan Holloway of Oldbury, who met their deaths in an explosion of gunpowder on board the *Tilbury* caused by ignition and vapour of benzene by fire or light in the cabin. Grand Junction Canal Company was found guilty of gross negligence and was fined accordingly. From Wednesday 14 October GJCC stopped carrying gunpowder altogether. Because of all safety requirements, the company had to charge twice the normal rate for carrying gunpowder

The remains of the Macclesfield Bridge after the explosion. It was known as 'Blow-up Bridge' after rebuilding. (Waterscape/ BW)

and they were fearful of impending compensation claims from the families. Recently, claims have been made that on board the *Tilbury* a young woman may have been the cause of the explosion as it believed that she was cooking for all seven boats. Her body was found after the explosion but her identity remains unknown and she was buried in an unmarked grave.

2

CANAL DEATHS

On 17 June 1839 a woman of thirty-seven, Christina Collins, *née* Brown, was viciously murdered by some boatmen who had been drinking in a local pub. She was the passenger on their Pickfords & Co. boat travelling down to London to join her husband, Robert Collins, with their chattels, which would explain why she was aboard a removal boat.

Christiana Brown as she was christened, or Christina as she liked to be called, was born on 17 July 1801 in Nottingham and came from a relatively prosperous family. Her father invented machines related to the Nottingham lace trade. All was going well for the family until a business venture failed

The murder of Christina Collins.

and by 1818, the year he died, her father was receiving parish relief. After her father's death her mother was forced into employment as a nurse, a path followed by Christina, until she met and married her first husband, Thomas Ingleby. He was a travelling conjuror and Christina assisted him. He had a wide repertoire of tricks and used the title 'Emperor of Conjurors', going on to write a book on the subject. In 1832 Ingleby died in Ireland leaving Christina a small sum of money that allowed her to get home to her mother. She married Robert Collins, an ostler (stable man) in 1838, and they moved to Liverpool so that he could look for work. Christina found work quickly but, after weeks of looking, Robert decided to depart to London for a job he had been offered there. Soon he found accommodation and sent a guinea for Christina's fare to London, and she secured passage on a narrowboat. This was the start of the tragedy that became known as the Bloody Steps Murder.

Christina's money was subsequently found along with a letter in one of her trunks on board the narrowboat. In the letter her husband had written that he wished her to make haste to him, as he was feeling lonely and missed her. Only two days into the journey from Preston Brook the crew had become aware of the beautiful Christina, who habitually walked along the towpath or hid in her small cabin away from the drunken men. On the day of her death she wore a dark-coloured gown with a blue silk bonnet held to her head by a ribbon fastened under her chin. The men had become adept at stealing spirits from the barrels they were carrying, and on this occasion became more and more drunk as they travelled down the canal. Three of the men went off to the local pub and drank heavily before returning to the boat where Christina had cooked them an evening meal. Some time later three men went into her small sleeping area and dragged her into the covered hold. There they stripped some of her clothing from her and forced a series of violent and repeated rapes and sexual acts upon her. Exhausted by their attack, Christina managed to get out on deck but there she had her throat cut and her body was thrown into the Trent and Mersey Canal at Brindley Steps. Her screams of terror were heard coming from the direction of the lock at midnight by the keeper of Hoo Mill lock, James Mills and his wife, Anne. Looking out of their cottage window they saw three men and a woman on the boat. Worried for the safety of the woman, Mills dressed and went to the lock where he spoke to one of the men, George Thomas, who assured him she was a passenger and her husband was on board.

At 1.30a.m. on Monday, a boatman passed Thomas and Owen who were looking into the canal. Trying to cover the murder, they asked if he had seen a woman, explaining their passenger had gone missing. He had not, so sailed on. At 5a.m., as her sodden body was pulled from the canal, a flow of blood oozed from her wound and trickled down the sandstone steps to the canal, known as the Bloody Steps. The body was taken to the Talbot Inn (long since demolished) where it was placed in an outbuilding. The four men were caught trying to escape on their boats when a lock keeper called in the police as he was not satisfied with their description of what had happened. They were arrested and sent to trial on three counts of rape, murder and theft. The trial went on for many days and was recorded in various newspapers which produced many illustrations of the trial and then a flysheet covering the day of the hanging. The first offence of rape was dropped as the body had been in the water too long and showed little sign of attack other than bruising on the inner thighs. This contradicted the first doctor and attendant's opinions as her underclothes were ripped or missing (the men did confess later to the act). Three of the men, James Owen, George Thomas and William Ellis, were convicted of murder. The judge passed sentence:

> James Owen, George Thomas and William Ellis, after a long and patient hearing of the circumstances of this case, and after due deliberation on the part of the jury, you have been found guilty of the foul crime of murder, murder on an unoffending and helpless woman who was under your protection and who, there is reason to believe, was the object of your lust; and then, to prevent detection for that crime, was the object of your cruelty. Not for pardon in this world. Apply to the God of Mercy for that pardon which He alone can extend to penitent sinners, and prepare yourselves for the ignominious death which await you. This case is one of the most shocking that has ever come under my knowledge, and it remains for me to pass upon you the awful sentence of the law, that you be taken from whence you came, and from thence to the place of execution, and that you, and each of you, be hanged by the neck until you are dead, and that your bodies afterwards be buried within the precincts of the prison. And may God have mercy on your souls.

The evening before his execution was due, Ellis had his sentence commuted to being transported to Australia for life, but after further intervention this was reduced to fourteen years. He went to Australia, where he lived the rest of his life. The young lad Musson was not charged and was given alibis by the other three.

Hanging after Christina Collin's murder. (Rugeley Town archive)

Christina Collins was buried in Rugeley, where her grave stands proudly in Rugeley church with a dedication from the local community which reads:

To the memory of Christina Collins wife of Robert Collins, London who having been most barbarously treated was found dead in the canal in this parish on June 17, 1899 aged 37 years. This stone was erected by some individuals of the parish of Rugeley in commiseration of the end of this unhappy woman.

 Murderers have, since the opening of the canals, used the waterways in an attempt to hide their wicked act. On 2 February 1837 a workman found a pair of legs in a field in Brixton which were to complete a body whose first part, the headless torso, was discovered at Pineapple Tollgate building development in Edgware Road in December 1836. In January the head appeared, blocking a lock gate on the Regent's Canal in Stepney. Later the woman was identified as the launderer Hannah Brown. She had been expected to marry James Greenacre on Christmas Day. On Christmas Eve, however, Greenacre informed their friends that the wedding had been cancelled as neither he nor Hannah had the money to set up home together. Hannah had not been seen since Christmas Eve. Greenacre's neighbours in Camberwell noticed that he spent the week over Christmas working behind closed doors and curtains and then he too disappeared. Greenacre was finally discovered in bed with his mistress Sarah Gale in Lambeth, who was wearing earrings belonging to Hannah Brown. In her defence Sarah, who had been with Greenacre, had quietly left the Camberwell house just after Miss Brown arrived for a pre-wedding supper on Christmas Eve and so could only be charged as an accessory after the fact. Greenacre claimed that there'd been a massive quarrel when they discovered that they were both penniless as they both believed the other had money from a private source. He claimed that in the fight he picked up a silk weaving roller and in self-defence hit her on the head, which threw her back on to the fireplace where she dashed her head and was dead. In panic, he claimed during the court case, he'd dismembered the body and dumped pieces in far-flung places to avoid being caught. The jury found him guilty of murder and of dissection and he was hanged in 1837. His last letter from prison warned his children against the perils of greed.

 A week before John Gurd was due to marry Florence Adams she announced that she had changed her mind and didn't want to marry him after all. Gurd, twenty-nine, was completely shocked and decided that it must have been Henry Richards, Florence's uncle, who had put her up to ending the relationship. On 9 April 1892 he met up with Richards for a drink in a local pub in Melksham. He wanted to put his case forward that he would make a good husband to Florence. As they strolled along the Kennet and Avon Canal bank the pair started to argue. Gurd pulled out a pistol and shot Richards twice, once in the head and once in the chest, before throwing the body into the canal. He ran from the scene when a number of people from nearby working boats rushed towards him in an attempt to apprehend the murderer. Some hours later he ended up outside an inn near Warminster in the middle of the night. He tried to break into the pub but when the landlord came to the window with a shotgun and threatened to shoot him, Gurd fled. The police were summoned; Gurd was found close by

Greenacre murdering
Hannah Brown.

hiding near the entrance to Longleat Park. He fired two shots, one of which hit Police Sergeant Enos Molden who died shortly afterwards in hospital. Gurd was eventually overpowered and at his trial pleaded insanity due to the emotional stress the breakup had caused. On 26 July 1892 in Devizes Prison, Gurd was hanged for the murder of Richards and Sgt Molden.

Some acts of murder start with infatuation, as happened with Joseph Heffermann who, after leaving the country to find work in the town of Mullingar, County Westmeath, found lodgings close to a young woman and took an instant shine to her. Heffermann felt sure that Mary Walker had feelings for him when she found him a job at the post office, where she worked as a telephonist. They often walked to work together and had been seen out in a group, fuelling Heffermann's belief that they were a couple. However, after starting work he failed to win Mary's heart and it soon became clear she was hoping for one of the postmen to woo her. When Heffermann was sacked she hoped he would leave her alone, as he was often seen sending her notes and small gifts. A few days after leaving the job Heffermann ambushed Mary as she walked home across the bridge over Lacy's Canal and dragged her down on to the towpath. The couple were heard arguing by a number of witnesses. The date was 8 July 1909, and when Heffermann staggered into his lodgings, shouting to his landlady that he had seen a woman murdered on the towpath, she put it down to him being blind drunk. A search for Walker was carried out after she failed to return to her lodgings; her landlady's son found Walker's body on the canal towpath, her throat slit so deeply her head was thrust back in the bushes.

The next day Heffermann's landlady asked him to fix a new handle to her broom which he had managed to break when he fell in the lavatory in a drunken state. As he trimmed the top of the handle to fix the head she noticed his whittling knife was covered in blood. News was quick to race around the town and when Heffermann's landlady heard how Mary had died she went straight to the police with her worries about her lodger, explaining he had been acting very peculiarly. Then other witnesses came forward with pieces of information that led to Heffermann being charged with the murder of Mary Walker. The trial was swift and despite his plea that he was insane at the time of the murder, he was sentenced to death. He was hanged on 4 January 1910 in Dublin.

Shortly after the Rochdale Canal was filled with water in 1798 there occurred the first of many drownings. Between Gauxholme and Gauxholme Stones a body was pulled from the strangely clear water. Ely Crossley had a small farm at Gauxholme and enjoyed the company of friends at local inns along the canal. Being a man of habit, it appears that he had taken the route of the old road that had been moved so the route of the canal could remain straight, the newly altered road now running alongside the canal. When he failed to arrive home the family went out to search for him,

Location of Mary Walker's death at the hands of Heffermann.

yet he was nowhere to be seen and they thought he must be sleeping the drink off in a hedge somewhere, which he often did. The next morning, however, his body was found in the canal. Drinkers at the inn had said they heard him argue with a man called Eastwood from a farm nearby over the price of a cow. It appears that Eastwood, still arguing with Ely, had followed him down the new road. When they reached Copperas House Bridge there was a struggle, at which point Ely fell into the canal where he drowned as Eastwood looked on and gave no assistance. Ely left a wife and seven children at his untimely death. The case against Eastwood never came to court. Ely was buried at St Mary's church in October 1798.

Adrian Sutcliffe of Scout was going home on a Saturday night after spending time in the pub carrying a heavy load of wraps and weft for looms he operated at home. Crossing the ice-covered lock gates, he slipped and banged his head as he fell into the water. He had no chance of survival as the wraps and weft were strung over his shoulders and he quickly went to the bottom. It was only when the lock was opened the next day that his body come floating out. He was buried on 27 December 1821, shortly followed by his wife Sally, who died a few weeks later of a broken heart. They left behind nine children who ended up with relatives or in the workhouse.

Close to this tragedy there was a mystery drowning that happened at Gauxholme on 10 November 1833, when William Woodhead was found drowned in the same place that his mother drowned some thirteen years earlier. It was rumoured that he had been depressed and perhaps took his own life.

Some three years later, in November 1836, the body of John Walton, the gamekeeper who covered the shooting grounds over the moors of Todmorden and Walston, was dragged from the Rochdale Canal at Birks Mill in Walsden. He and his wife had not been getting on for some time and he had stormed out on a Wednesday afternoon and visited many pubs, fellow drinkers saying that when he left he was the worse for drink. He stayed out all night, possibly in someone's shed or a barn, yet by two o'clock the next afternoon he was back in the pubs he visited the day before. By ten o'clock in the evening he was so drunk that a landlord forced him out of the pub and told him to go home. That was the last time he was seen alive. He left a wife and five small children.

When newspapers became popular they were used to convey all kinds of messages and announcements, even sometimes being used to find missing people, as with the *Leeds Mercury* on 20 November 1843:

Missing – a person the name of Joshua Feilden of Bottoms, aged 60, has left his home on Friday evening the 10th of November about six o'clock, and has not been since been heard of. He has frequently shown symptoms of derangement, and some time ago attempted to cut his own throat, though not effectively. A short time before he left home that day, and while sitting at tea with his wife, he told her it was the last time he would eat, and that he knew a place where he could hide himself, and where no one would find him. They have searched the canal and the mill dams in the neighbourhood, but no clues have yet been found to mysterious affair. The missing individual has a large scar or mark on the left side of his head that reaches to the back part of, caused by tread of a horse, and left home without a hat, having on brown fustian coat and waistcoat, drab cotton cord trousers, and a pair of clogs on its feet. It would be an act of greatest kindness and compassion of anyone transmitting to his disconsolate friends any intelligence respecting him.

Unfortunately he did find somewhere to hide, for on 11 December Joshua Feilden was found drowned in the Light Bank lock.

It would seem that alcohol and canals do not mix, as the next story proves. A timber merchant, James Howarth, also known as 'Old Jock' Todmorden, went missing on 7 February 1850. On 11 February his body was found in the canal opposite the Sun Inn at Walston; he was fifty-six and previously had been landlord of the Woodstock Inn, Walston. The *Manchester Times* on Saturday 16 February 1850 recorded, under the title 'Melancholy Event', that on Friday Mr James Howarth, a timber merchant, had gone missing after drinking at the Wagon and Horses, Willesden. Some believed that he was away on business, buying wood or catching up with his many contacts whilst others felt sure he had slipped into the canal and perished. On the Sunday following the disappearance his hat was found on the bank opposite the Sun Inn at Walton along his route home. Police Sergeant Heap gave orders for the canal in that area to be dredged. Late into Sunday night they searched in vain. On Monday the sergeant asked the canal company to lower the water level in the side ponds, which they did. At 7p.m. Howarth's body was discovered in Dean Royd pool. The body was removed to rest in the tap room of the Lord Nelson, which hosted the inquest that Wednesday. The coroner recorded a verdict of 'Found Drowned'.

Drink was not always to blame when people died along the canals and Rochdale Canal has had its share of accidental deaths. On 3 November 1850, local grocer Mr Henry Lacy, aged seventy-four, was pulled from the canal between Todmorden and Walston. He was a sober man and it was believed that he had slipped and fallen into the canal, for when his body was pulled from the cold waters he was found to have £2 8s 2d in his pockets. The coroner recorded a verdict of 'Found Drowned'. Boatmen also drowned, as happened to Samuel Butterworth. On 21 February 1860, he had been taking a boat through the locks singlehandedly at Hollins lock tail. He must have slipped and fallen under the boat for some time later another boatman tried to enter the lock. Realising he needed to move the seemingly abandoned boat, he opened the lock gates and it was only when Butterworth's boat was moved out of the lock that his body floated to the top.

Canals are often scenes of frolics and such reckless action can result in death, as happened to one young man who, despite his friends pleading him to follow them home on the towpath, ran off towards a lock gate in late April 1850. Eli Sutcliffe, twenty-three, was employed by Ashton & Co., mechanics of Salford. He left the factory with colleagues to have a drink as they walked home, part of the route being the canal towpath. Sutcliffe was the worse for drink and had been running along the towpath at speed daring his friends to do the same. When the group arrived at the lock near the Todmorden Wharf, Sutcliffe jumped on to the top lock gate and started to cross to the other side. As he did so his friends shouted for him to stop and come back to them. Perhaps their shouts distracted him or perhaps the drink took over; either way he lost his footing and fell into the canal. Every effort was made to find him and pull him from the water but to no avail. After an hour of frantic searching with a pole and hook, Sergeant Heap found Sutcliffe's body, which was removed to the Golden Lion Inn. His young wife attended the inquest the following Saturday, where a verdict of 'Accidentally Drowned' was returned.

Children also have a fascination for water and sometimes become victims of it too. The *Leeds Mercury* reported: 'a child about four years old, daughter of Mr John Wade, chemist, was playing by the side of the canal and fell in and was drowned. She was almost immediately rescued, and every means used to restore animation, but in vain.'

Another young person fell through the ice that covered the canal in December 1864. The body of sixteen-year-old Mary Travis was a very sad sight to those who pulled her from the canal at Lane Bottom pool. She was a well-liked young woman who lived at Lock House with her family. She had been returning home from work and, it is believed, slipped on a patch of ice before falling into the canal and drowning under the ice.

Whilst accidents often occurred due to drink, ice or slippery surfaces on bridges and towpaths, some have used canal waters to commit suicide. In March 1851 Robert Taylor, an engineer of Hayward, went missing and had not been seen for over a week after leaving the Bird in Hand in Walston a little bit worse for wear. He was thirty-nine years of age and was found drowned in the canal at Walston. Another man who apparently committed suicide, who is still unknown, was found drowned below what is known as the Punchbowl. On the side of the canal were left a hat, items of clothing and an unsigned letter begging a sweetheart's forgiveness, with a penny on top. It was assumed that the penny was for the cost of posting the letter on 11 April 1851. A police note accompanied the original letter asking the person who received it to get in touch with them. Although the letter was delivered, the intended recipient had long since vanished from the lodgings.

Williams Southwell, alias Billy Sixpence, was helping to unload a boat one evening at locks at Gauxholme wharf. Having taken his fair share of beer allowance as payment, he decided to walk to the next town to buy a toy as a present for his grandson. Having done that, he returned to the canal, heading to the Black Bull for another drink. Instead of crossing by the bridge he opted to use the shortcut, which was a plank, across the lower lock. He fell in and his body was discovered the next morning, 27 December 1880, floating in the canal, the toy still in his hand.

Often bodies are left undisturbed as they are mistaken for dead animals or bundles of floating rubbish. On 28 April 1898, when Matthew Wadsworth of Walston was working on the canal bank below Pinnel lock, his attention was caught by something in the water. Initially thinking he'd seen a dog, he was about to pass by when he looked again and realised it was in fact a man's body. He pulled the body to the side of the lock but the man was too heavy to be pulled out. He contacted the police who helped him heave the man from the water. Matthew Wadsworth thought that he could have been in the water eight or nine days from the look of him.

The dead man was a stranger and could not be identified initially. The man had nothing in his pockets apart from a tin containing a small amount of tobacco, a lead pencil and a smoking pipe. His body was unusual in that he was heavily tattooed. On the left side, his inner forearms were tattooed with representations of two ladies in theatrical costume and both wrists had braces tattooed upon them, as well as other tattoos including an anchor and heart pierced with an arrow. On each hand, on the left-hand ankle and between the thumb and forefinger of the right hand he had a heart pierced by an arrow. As luck would have it, one of the men on the inquest jury was Thomas Sparks, who owned a lodging house on Butcher's Hill in Walston. He immediately recognised the stranger by his tattoos. He told the inquest the man had stayed at his lodging house several times, the last time being two weeks previously. He normally stayed up to three days at a time, a respectable man, not known to drink, and who liked to go to public houses in the evenings to sing. He was well dressed and appeared to want for nothing. He didn't know his name or where he normally lived, but knew he had been a soldier.

There were no marks of violence on the body, which was covered in thick mud when pulled from the canal. The jury returned an open verdict on the body, releasing it for burial. The relieving officer made arrangements for the body to be buried, but just in time someone came forward and identified him. It turned out that the deceased was Luke Crabtree of Burnley, where he had been employed as a gas stoker at the Burnley Gasworks. He left a widow and two children; the eldest was seven years old. The widow said her husband had been absent from home for about a fortnight. He was better known by the name of 'Ludlow'. Luke was buried at Christ Church in Todmorden.

 It is not always easy to tell whether drownings are accidental. On Wednesday night, 2 November 1848, Mr Abel Marland, Mr Ramsden Wood and Mrs Sarah Priestley, wife of William Priestley, were seen together at a late hour in Todmorden at the Nelson Inn. Being neighbours, it appears that Marland and Priestley agreed to go home together as the night was dark. When they got to Copperas House Bridge they headed off up the wet bank and slipped into the canal below. Marland clambered out then saw that Priestley was still in the water so jumped in and pulled her to the side, but was unable to get her out. Calling for assistance, he was assisted by residents nearby but she was found to be quite dead. At the inquest into the death of Sarah Priestley, aged fifty, the circumstances surrounding events that night and Marland's role in the situation were discussed. The coroner gave Marland a severe telling off, saying: 'there was not sufficient evidence to warrant his committal, it did not exonerate him in the eye of the public, as to his foul and disgraceful intentions in persuading, even allowing, the deceased to go by such a dangerous route in the dead of night.' Mr Feilden cautioned him to be more careful of his conduct in future. The village was rife with suggestions that Sarah was taken to the spot with the intention of murder.

There seemed to be no evidence of an affair but Marland was known to be a ladies' man and the two were known to have spent time together.

Oddingley is a small village between Worcester and Droitwich through which the Worcester and Birmingham Canal runs. Oddingley was the scene of two murders in June 1806. A local carpenter, Richard Hemmings, shot the Revd G. Parker, the rector of the parish of St James, at point-blank range.

Hemmings was never seen alive again. He was known to be a violent man and to have fallen into debt after gambling with a group of four local men; a debt he was unable to pay. Why had he brutally murdered the Revd G. Parker, who was an unpopular man but who had helped Hemmings and his family in the past? Parker was disliked by many of the richer people in the parish for extracting every penny of tithe tax he could, and was even known to take livestock without consent to sell at market if he felt a full tithe had not been paid to him, and because he had God on his side, he got away with it. Four local men – Clewes, Banks, Bennett and Taylor – hatched a plan to get rid of the reverend once and for all. They hired Hemmings to commit the murder as a way of paying off his gambling debt to them. The plan was set. As Parker drove a herd of cows down a narrow lane for milking, Hemmings would shoot him and then go into hiding for a few weeks. All went to plan and the reverend was fatally shot by Hemmings, who had hidden in nearby bushes waiting for the cows to pass. Leaving his gun behind as part of the plan, Hemmings doubled back to the village in order to make good his escape with the help of the others, who by now had heard the killing was a success. Clewes persuaded Hemmings to hide in the hayloft of his barn at Netherwood Farm. The conspirators were afraid that Hemmings would tell of their involvement and agreed that he would have to die. Clewes, Banks, Bennett and Taylor lured him out of his hiding place with the offer of food and beer. As soon as he was in sight, they set about him, beating him to death before burying him under the floor of the old barn.

Once the reverend's body was discovered the musket was recognised as Hemmings' and a wide search was ordered to apprehend the killer. After a few days, the search was halted and it was locally assumed that he had fled the country. However, the four left were implicated in the murder after Clewes confessed after many sleepless nights and the thought of God's wrath, but despite his confession the other three denied murder and were all acquitted due to lack of evidence. An inquest was held at the Talbot Inn in nearby Barbourne, Worcester. On a cold winter's day some twenty-four years later, the body of Hemmings was found buried under the floor of the barn at Netherwood Farm. In the neighbouring hamlet of Dunhampstead, the Fir Tree Inn can be found by the railway crossing close to the canal; it is a popular inn and one that hides a sinister past linked to the murders at Ottingley. Just months after murdering Hemmings, Thomas Clewes became the landlord of the inn and the public bar is known locally as the 'murderer's bar'.

It is an offence to impersonate a police officer for many reasons, not least of which is the ease with which a criminal can take advantage of the public's trust, as the next recorded murder shows. Olive Turner and Charles Broomhead had known each other some nine months and had been going out together for six weeks. On 2 July 1927 Charles had taken his lady to the cinema in Winson Green Road, Birmingham. The film finished at 9.40p.m. and Charles began to walk Olive home to Ford Street, Hockley. As they passed the entrance to the canal towpath, eighteen-year-old Olive suggested a walk along the side of the canal for a change, saying it would be romantic. They slowly walked along the canal and saw a couple standing close to the asylum wall. Soon afterwards, Olive stopped with the intention of kissing Charles. At this point a large, well-built man strode towards them from the direction of the High Street, told them he was a police officer and informed the couple they were trespassing on private property. He asked their names and addresses, which they gave quite readily even though he showed no form of identification. He then asked them for proof of who they were. As the man asked more questions Olive became increasingly upset. She told him she was an orphan and begged to be released as the questioning was really upsetting for her. Charles even offered to go to the police station with the policeman so that Olive could get on her way home. The policeman stated that it could all be put right for money. Charles looked in his pockets and grabbed four pennies which he showed to the policeman who dismissed such a small amount.

Charles and Olive became convinced that he was not a real policeman and that they needed a way out. As the man escorted them down the canal towpath they passed two other couples leaning against walls and kissing. Why was he not arresting them, Charles asked. The man said he already had two suspects so that was enough for the night. Charles then urged Olive to run for it towards Clissold Street which she did but the man dashed after her. Charles was fast himself and managed to get ahead of the man quite quickly, but as he pushed Olive up towards the steps into the High Street the man grabbed Charles from behind, pulled him towards him and thumped him in the face before throwing him down on the ground, dazed. He reported later that he was only down for what he thought was a few minutes yet when he pulled himself up and looked around there was no sign of Olive or the man.

He searched high and low but couldn't find her and eventually ran up to Olive's home in Ford Street. There he met James Rooke, who was courting Olive's sister. Together they returned to the canal and renewed their search. Now close to midnight, they soon found her hat and a handbag near a bridge. As it was late they decided they would need the police. Birmingham police force searched on 3 July and eventually recovered Olive's body from the dark waters of the Soho branch of the canal. Her wristwatch showed that it stopped at 11.41p.m., the time of her death. Charles was initially the chief suspect; however, when the police appealed for witnesses a number came forward who said that they had also seen a tall gentleman standing on the canal towpath harassing young couples as they walked towards Western Road Bridge. A boatman, John Godfrey, was sailing his boat at 10.30p.m. on 2 July in the area when he recalled seeing a muscular man going up to a courting couple and from his attitude he assumed that he was a policeman. He stopped a couple who quickly walked away from him and he then moved on to the next couple. One couple who came forward, John Whillock and his girlfriend Doris Emeny, had been to the cinema and were walking back to Doris' house in Winson Green Road along the towpath. By the old workhouse they noticed a tall man talking to a woman who was holding hands with a shorter man. They could not hear precisely what was said but clearly heard the chink of money. A little later the girl they had seen, Olive, came running toward them breathlessly and cried they must hurry with her to escape. John and Doris ran with the girl towards Main Street but close to the bridge the tall man they'd seen caught up with them. He grabbed Olive's shoulder, at which point she fainted away and he grabbed her around the waist to support her. John was not a man to turn away from any situation so he asked the tall man what he wanted with the woman, to which he replied that he was a policeman and Olive was being arrested. Believing him, John and Doris walked away. The 'policeman' then took the semi-conscious Olive under the bridge, so this was the last time she was seen alive. When John and Doris later saw a photograph of Olive Turner they realised it was the same girl they had witnessed being caught by the tall man.

Another witness, Florence Robinson, said that she was walking home after a whist drive and was on the bridge over the canal at 11.35p.m., when she heard terrifying screams from the canal side. She assumed they came from a patient in the mental hospital nearby. Another witness, Frank Pritchett, who was in his bedroom in Brookfield Road at 11.42p.m., heard horrible screams coming from the canal but could not see anyone. One witness who was to prove very helpful was Caroline Leonard. At 11.45p.m. she was looking out of her kitchen window when she saw a man jump over the canal wall and drop down into the alleyway. She described him as tall, very broad, wearing a dark coat and lighter-coloured hat pulled down to cover part of his face. A similar description was also given by Thomas Hill, walking down the canal on his way home from the Theatre Royal at about 11.10p.m. He also saw a tall man talking to a young couple who fitted the description Charles gave to the police. Police issued a statement that they were looking for a man about 5ft 10in, well built, clean shaven with dark hair and dark suit and a dirty light collar, walking splay-footed with a swinging gait.

The inquest was opened on 5 July by Mr Isaac Bradley. Basic evidence was given that the police had no evidence to link a killer to the murder. At the inquest Detective Sergeant Albert Edwards looked at the description of the man and felt that he had been a serving officer and at some point

Olive Turner.

had been dismissed. In Kenyon Street there was a canning factory in which it was believed the suspect worked. Between 6p.m. and 6.45p.m. ninety men and boys left the factory. Broomhead watched them all from a parked car. Not one of them was the man he saw, and then suddenly, a few minutes later, he saw the man who had stopped them on the towpath. At the same time the suspect recognised Broomhead and ran back into the factory. There was a chase and James Joseph Power was taken into custody. He was interviewed and then charged with the murder of Olive Turner. Power was put before an identification parade at the police station but only one witness identified him. Because of this he felt there was no case to answer against him so it should be dismissed. The magistrate did not agree and Power was remanded for one week.

On 13 July Power was charged with impersonating a police officer and demanding money with menaces, which gave them a separate hearing at a future date. He was back before the magistrates on 19 July on the charge of demanding money with menaces from Charles Broomhead and Olive Turner. Detective Sgt Edwards told the court that when cautioned in Kenyon Street, Power replied, 'I was never near the cut that night'. He stated he was at a cricket match at Cape Hill with his friend Jack Davies, that after the match had finished they spent the evening in the public house. The two friends had finally parted on the corner of Heath Green Road at 10.45p.m. and Power had gone home. Mr Davies confirmed most of the story except the time, saying that he had left Power at 10.25p.m., not 10.45p.m., which led to Power being remanded again until 21 July. This went on and on until 3 August, when Power was informed of another charge, that of raping a woman on the canal side at Winson Green.

The rape charge related to an incident on 23 May at 10.45p.m. in the same area of the canal towpath that Olive was murdered, when Lucy Folks, a widow, was walking with her new man, Thomas Pit. A man approached them and said he was a police officer; the couple had no identification so Power suggested that money might change hands in order for him to let them go. Pit was out of work and had no money and could not pay up, and at that he was put into an armlock by Power, forced to the ground and then shook by the neck until he passed out. He regained consciousness and finally arrived home at 1.30a.m. He assumed that Lucy had found her way home because he couldn't find her along the canal towpath. He hadn't realised that Power had grabbed Lucy and taken her under the bridge some distance along the canal and raped her repeatedly. She had not told anyone about her ordeal until she heard about the assault on 7 July, when she read about the death of Olive Turner. Both Thomas and Lucy attended the parade and they immediately picked out Power as the man who had attacked them.

On 11 August Power was sent to trial for charges of murder, demanding money with menaces, assault and rape. The proceedings went on until 9 December, with the most serious charge of murder taking precedence over the others. As the witnesses told their stories the case had built up against Power. At the closing statement Power launched an attack upon Sgt Edwards, saying that he still maintained the jury and the witnesses had made an honest mistake. He tried to convince the jury that Sgt Edwards arrived at the prison to serve some additional evidence on him, and had proceeded to attack him in his cell. An appeal was entered and heard on 13 January 1928, and once again the defence made much of the discrepancy in the evidence; however, Lord Hewart, the Lord Chief Justice, stated that in the opinion of the court there was corroboration of the statements made since the appeal and it was dismissed. On Tuesday 31 January 1928 at Winson Green Prison, some 600 yards from the spot where Olive Turner had met her death, James Joseph Power was hanged by Thomas Pierrepoint, the famous hangman, assisted by Robert Wilson, whilst outside the prison a group of 2,000 people waited to read the notice that the execution had taken place.

Long before the canals were built there were still murders along their routes. One such murder took place on the line of the Montgomery Canal, where stands a former lock-keeper's cottage at Burgedin. Close to this spot a young couple were murdered by a vengeful father. The Welsh princess Eira was caught running away with her lover, who was an outlaw. The king was so angry with them that the couple was bricked up in the alcoves of the cellar of his hunting lodge, shackled in chains with one brick removed at eye level so they could hear and see the other perish from starvation in their tomb. A guard was placed at the door with orders to kill anyone who tried to free them – even the queen – such was the king's anger.

More recently, canals have been used by criminals to hide evidence of their crimes. In 1935, a woman's torso was discovered floating in the Grand Union Canal at Brentford. On the same day, the legs of a woman were found in a railway carriage at Waterloo. There was an extensive search for the rest of the body but no other body parts were found and to date no one knows who she was.

Canals have been used as a method of quietly moving large quantities of stolen goods. Coal, or black gold as it was sometimes known, was very saleable and is still a commodity targeted by thieves. In London's Curzon Street entire sacks of coal were being stolen and so a detective officer with the London and North Western Railway police force was on patrol on 10 August 1901. His name was Hibs. By now the canals and the railways were often working in partnership to keep the delivery of coal to the many locations that steam engines required. Hibs was on patrol when he spotted three shadowy characters moving from the coal yard down towards the Regent's Canal. Hibs watched for a while to make sure they were stealing coal and then challenged the men to stop. There were three of them who turned towards him and, before he could raise his whistle to his mouth and bring out his truncheon, they attacked him with such force to render him unconscious. As if a sack of coal, they must have lifted Hibs up to shoulder height before throwing him into the canal, where in his unconscious state he drowned. The London and North Western Railway & Canal Company offered a reward of £100, yet despite the offer the case remains unsolved.

 Another criminal, George Ball, was a twenty-two-year-old tarpaulin packer who, aided by eighteen-year-old Samuel Elltoft, murdered his employer and disposed of the body in the Leeds and Liverpool Canal. On 10 December 1913 a ship's steward was waiting for his girlfriend outside the tarpaulin maker's shop in Old Hall Street, Liverpool. He saw a young lad come out of the shop pushing a handcart with a bundle on it. The lad was soon joined by another lad and the two walked off down the street pushing the cart and load. The steward had just unknowingly witnessed the disposal of a murder victim's body. The body of forty-year-old Christina Bradfield had been stuffed inside the sack and was then discarded into the waters of the canal nearby. It was found the following day in one of the lock gates and, when examined, was found to have been battered with several savage blows from a blunt instrument. A manhunt was quickly launched for the two men. The police had no difficulty finding Elltoft, who was found at home in bed, but Ball had vanished. The manhunt continued for a further ten days before he was discovered in a lodgings house in the city. Although Ball denied the charge, his bloodstained clothing gave him away. He was tried and convicted of murder at Liverpool Assizes and was hanged by John Ellis on 26 February 1914 in Liverpool. Elltoft was found not guilty of murder but guilty of being an accessory after the fact. Elltoft was given four years' penal servitude for his involvement in the disposal of the body.

 It is a little-known fact that both William Burke and William Hare worked on the (New) Union Canal near Edinburgh. This was where they started their life of crime and a location in which Hare ruthlessly dispatched rivals through bare-knuckle fighting or just a lead cosh about the head before dropping the corpse into the puddle clay or canal waters.

Hare was born in Newry, Ireland, and emigrated to Scotland to work on the Union Canal, though he did not meet Burke at that time. They later realised that one or two of the people Hare had removed from life they had previously both known as fellow navvies on the canal. Hare settled in the West Port area of Edinburgh and lodged with Margaret Logue and her husband, soon beginning an affair with Margaret. There was an inevitable fight and some believe that Hare murdered Margaret's husband, who was found dead the day after he had caught his wife and their new lodger making love in his matrimonial bed and had thrown them out of the lodging. As there was no proof that Hare had committed a crime and the local population were terrified of him, he was left a free man and moved in with Margaret to run the lodging house.

William Burke was born in Orrey, County Tyrone, into a poor Catholic family where he lived until he reached eighteen years of age, working as a weaver and then a manservant to a local gentleman. When the gentleman died Burke joined the Donegal militia where he remained for five years. He married in County Mayo and his wife bore him seven children, all but one of whom died in infancy. At some point the marriage broke down and he left for employment on the construction of the Union Canal near Edinburgh where he met a woman named Helen McDougall. Soon after that meeting they agreed to live as man and wife. They moved to Edinburgh and engaged in petty crimes in order to make a living, from selling old clothing and shoes to stealing washing from lines to sell. As times were hard they moved away from Edinburgh for a short period to work on a farm but came back after the harvest of 1827, where they met William Hare at the lodging house in Tanners Close, West Port. It was here that the infamous pair bonded over a shared lust for money and worked out how to obtain it by providing cadavers for the Dr Robert Knox at the local hospital.

Their first transaction involved an old man called Desmond. He died naturally in the lodging house yet gave them a decent profit on his debt of £3 10s (£3.50) when they sold his body to Knox for £7 10s. From then on these plotters lured poor unfortunates into the lodging house, where these victims were plied with copious amounts of gin or whisky and then smothered as they lay in a drunken stupor. From December 1827 to October 1828 they murdered three men, twelve women and one child aged just ten. Their victims were often recorded only by their trade or state of being as often they had no known names. After Desmond they went on to murder Joseph, a miller; Abigail Simpson, a salt peddler; an unnamed beggar from the Gilmorton area; an English match seller; an unnamed drunken old woman; Mary Patterson, who apparently enjoyed the company of many men in exchange for money; Margaret Haldane, a beggar; Effy, a well-known rubbish scavenger; a second drunken old woman, unnamed; and soon afterwards a drunken Irish woman and her deaf mute grandson of ten years old; and finally a laundry woman known as Mrs Ostler.

Burke even murdered Margaret's granddaughter, Margaret Haldane, when she began asking too many questions. They told Margaret she had met a man and left whilst Margaret was away tending to a sick relative. Thus the killing went on uninterrupted, Hare murdering a cousin of Helen's ex-husband named Anne McDougal and later that same day 'Daft' Jamie Wilson, whose body was the catalyst for the search for the killers after he was recognised by students dissecting the body. Before they were caught Burke and Hare also murdered an old Irish woman, Margery Docherty.

A police constable visited the lodgings following accusations that Burke and Hare had been offing their clients. He was reluctant to arrest them outright and asked them to accompany him to the police station where it turned out their stories did not match. Hare was the first to crack under further questioning and he turned King's Evidence against Burke, thus saving himself from hanging.

On 28 January 1829 Burke was publicly executed in Edinburgh. His body was publicly dissected two days later and the skeleton put on display in the Edinburgh Medical School with a book bound in Burke's skin in the police museum.

Having fled to England without Helen, the last sighting of Hare alive was in Carlisle; where and when he died is unknown to date but with more access to censuses he may one day be found.

Dr Knox was never prosecuted as it was too difficult to prove that he knew he had purchased bodies of murder victims. He moved to London soon after the execution to work in a cancer hospital where he died in 1862.

The public outcry of utter disgust at the ease at which bodies were purchased by medical schools led to the 1832 Anatomy Act that allowed for unclaimed bodies from workhouses and prisons to be used for dissection as well as bodies given by relatives for the same, with the expense of burial being met by the medical school. The Act came about to prevent further such murders and to replace the 1752 Act that allowed the bodies of those executed to be dissected; as the numbers of executions decreased and demands for bodies to dissect was increasing, further provision of cadavers was needed and the 1832 Act was welcomed.

3

POOLS AND STANDING
WATER DEATHS

Any body of water can be used to murder or hide victims' bodies. On 2 April 1879 Charles Cox, a commercial traveller, was on his way towards Thornsby, approaching a pit pool, when he suddenly saw a man, Edwin Smart, standing by the pool with the body of a woman, Lucy Derrick, floating in front of him. He looked at Cox and said he'd just committed murder at which point Cox turned and ran to the next town, fearing for his own life, where he raised the alarm. Edwin Smart was taken into custody for committing the crime, claiming he'd done it for the hell of it. He did not know the woman as he chanced upon her whilst walking along the track that led to the local pits where he worked. Police found a razor and pocket knife covered in blood in his pockets when they searched him. Thirty-five-year-old Smart was sentenced to death on 25 April 1879 by Mr Justice Hawkins at Worcester Assizes. He was hanged on 12 May 1879 in Gloucester Prison by William Marwood.

Even shallow water, such as the water found in ditches, has played a part in murder. William Murphy, a labourer and former soldier from Leigh, Lancashire, was convicted of the murder of his estranged wife, Gwen Ellen Jones, at Holyhead on Christmas Day, 1909. Having left him the previous year to escape his violent temper, she took with her a few items and her two children from an earlier marriage, fleeing to her father's home in Bethesda, North Wales. Months later she moved on to Anglesey where she lived with friends. Murphy, who had sobered up, tracked her down but, after failing to persuade her to return home with him, raged, grabbed hold of her, cut her throat and threw her body into a drainage ditch, where she was found later that day floating face down. Murphy then walked to the nearest town, entered a church and gave himself up to the vicar. He was arrested and sent to trial in January 1910. He was hanged by Henry Pierrepoint, assisted by William Willis, on 15 February 1910 at Caernarvon.

 Close to the Suffolk town of Beccles, a similar murder took place. During the Second World War many murders went unsolved, so when the smallest clue turned up it was jumped upon. Leading Aircraftsman Arthur Hays failed to return to RAF Beccles after a dance in the town so some of his friends worried he may have had too much drink and fallen into a ditch or the river. Hays, a little bit worse for drink had in fact turned up at the women's quarters, where he was redirected by the duty corporal back to his own billets. Soon after, Hays met up with twenty-seven-year-old Radio Operator Winifred Evans, who was also stationed a RAF Beccles. It appears they had walked for a while in the night and then Hays may have tried to be amorous – but was rejected. Hays, in a fit of rage and drink, then brutally raped Winifred Evans before suffocating her and throwing the partially clothed body into a water-filled ditch close to the base at Ellough. He finally returned to his billets and fell asleep. On parade the next day with a hangover, Hays was identified by the corporal on duty the night before as being the man he had seen near the women's quarters. Hays was arrested by the military police before being handed over to the civilian police, where he was charged with murder. Although the evidence against him was circumstantial, what proved his downfall was a letter that Hays had written in his own hand purporting to be from the real killer. It contained details of how Winifred Evans had been murdered, something only the murderer would know. When the handwriting was checked it was realised that this anonymous letter was in fact from Hays himself. Court records state: 'After three days' hearing, LAC Arthur Hays (thirty-seven) of 22, Harold Street, Colne, Lancashire, was at Suffolk Assizes on Wednesday sentenced to death for the murder of Winifred Mary Evans (twenty-seven) of Harlesden, London, member of the WAAF, whose body was found in a ditch at Ellough, near Beccles.' Mr Justice Macnaghten, in summing up, described it 'as a more savage and horrible than any in my experience of crime'.

The prosecution had alleged that the woman had been attacked and assaulted, and, said the judge, treated with such savagery and violence that she was not able to breathe. An anonymous letter purporting to confess to the murder was read when the trial opened in Bury St Edmunds on

Monday. Addressed to the CO of an aerodrome and written in block capital letters, the letter declared that the man in the dock had been wrongfully accused of the crime. The letter bore a Norwich postmark. It read:

> Will you please give this letter to the solicitors for the airmen who is so wrongfully accused of murdering Winnie Evans. I want to state that I am the person responsible for the above-mentioned girl's death. I had arranged to meet her at the bottom of the road where the body was found, at midnight. When I arrived she was not there, so I waited some time and decided to walk down towards the WAAF quarters. Just before I reached this I heard a voice and stood close to the hedge. I heard footsteps. It proved to be an airman. I don't think he saw me. Then I saw someone I recognize as Winnie. She said I should not have come down to meet her. A WAAF friend had offered to go along with her as the airman was drunk and had lost his way she had her cycle with; no one will ever find this. She told me she could not stay long. I must have been mad and I don't know what happened. I know she struggled.

That statement ended by the writer saying that he covered up his tracks and got rid of his clothes, which were bloodstained. 'I shall be going overseas shortly. Please convey my humble apologies to the airman concerned.' Then, said the council, their case is that the document emanated from the prisoner. Mr John Flowers, KC, for the prosecution, said that according to the handwriting expert the block lettering was the same on leave forms filled in by Hays, who was taken to Norwich Prison after the arrest. Mr Flowers said that the case of prosecution was built on circumstantial evidence, which in calmative effect produced certainty that Hays was the man who killed the girl. Hays and Evans were stationed at the same place. The body of a girl, apparently raped and suffocated, was found in a ditch. After returning from a dance the girl had changed and left for her place on duty about five minutes after midnight. She was accompanied for a short distance by another girl, who, on returning to the station, switched on a light in the hut and saw a man, whom she later identified as the accused. He said he had lost his way and she told him to get out. The accused had been to Beccles, where he had attended the dance. Apparently he said he had been drinking, yet claimed he was sober. One of the men would say that it was between one and half-past one when the accused entered the hut on the station, which meant he had taken over an hour to travel the nine-tenths of a mile from the WAAF camp. His conduct was strange, for he did not show a light and went to bed; nothing was said. In the morning it was noticed that his civilian shoes were exceptionally dirty. He spent some time brushing his trousers and cleaning his shoes, and later he was seen cleaning his trousers with a trowel. Later, said counsel, the accused made a statement to the police in which he said that after leaving the WAAF camp he never passed a soul.

When the case resumed on Tuesday, Det. Chief Inspector Green of Scotland Yard produced the letter, printed in block letters in blue crayon, and printed matter on the watch tab which Hays admitted was his writing. The inspector said there were pencils of similar types in Norwich Prison. Superintendent Cherrill worked for many years in the comparison and identification of handwriting department of Scotland Yard and said it often happens that in block letters the characteristics were even more significant than in ordinary handwriting. Mr John Flowers, KC, asked Cherrill was it his expert opinion that the anonymous letter was written by the same person who printed letters on leave forms as Hays had done, or not. Superintendent Cherrill confirmed it was and, under cross-examination, Cherrill was asked how he came to his conclusions about the handwriting so he went on to describe some of the letters as seeming superficially different, but in essence the same.

Earlier the judge had asked for a plan of the aerodrome layout. What they were looking for was a red-brick path covered with mud and verification of whether walking on it would cause the accused's shoes to be coated in brick dust from the number of footpaths close to the murder scene, but this proved a red herring. Dr Eric Biddell, the pathologist of the East Suffolk and Ipswich Hospital, examined the body in the ditch, where he formed the opinion that she had to have been thrown or fallen into the ditch with force and then jumped on, pinned down and raped violently, and the compression of the chest caused asphyxia, which the water in the ditch did not help. Hays, in evidence, denied having murdered the girl or written the anonymous letter. He had been back from ten days' leave with his wife and three children for four days. He went to Beccles and had about three pints of mild and bitter and at another public house had five pints. He then went to a dance and lost his bicycle. It was his first night out in town so he said he never saw anything of the girl that night or any other night. Asked by the council why he went to the women's ablutions hut, he replied that he thought it was his own hut. He did not know there was another road from Beccles. He received directions, went straight to his hut and got there around 12.30a.m. He did not put the light on because it was not custom to do so unless on duty. Hays thought his pals were asleep.

Questioned about the anonymous letter, the accused said he had been imprisoned since 5 December and only left the prison when he was escorted to attend court. When his cross-examination resumed on Wednesday, Hays was asked by Mr Flowers: 'How do you account for blood on your tunic?'

The accused replied the only reason he could give was that on one occasion he went out with two men and one cut his hand in falling off a bicycle and he helped to get him up. It would have been last October. Mr Flowers, addressing the jury, said if anything else was needed to prove the case against the accused it was provided by the anonymous letter. Reading that part of the letter which stated that 'a WAAF had offered to go a long with Miss Evans as an airman who was drunk was ahead', Mr Flowers said nobody in the world could have put that in this letter, according to any reasonable view of the evidence, except this man. The judge told the jury that if they thought the statement made by the accused to the police might be true, he was entitled to be acquitted. The jury took forty minutes considering their verdict. When asked if he had any reason to give why sentence of death should not be passed on him Hays replied: 'God knows I am innocent of this vile crime. I know God will look after me. I am not afraid.' As he turned to go below he looked at the gallery, where his wife was sitting in floods of tears. In March 1945 Airman Arthur Hays was executed at Norwich Prison. There had been no executions at Norwich since 8 March 1938.

On 16 May 1891, the mutilated body of a boy was found floating inside a kit bag in Liverpool docks. The bag also contained a knife and a saw, which police proved to be the murder weapons. The victim turned out to be nine-year-old Nicholas Martin who had been murdered by John Conway, a marine fireman. The bag was traced to Conway and witnesses came forward to say they had seen him and the boy together shortly before the body was found. Conway later confessed to the crime, which he blamed on drink. He was hanged by James Berry on 20 August 1891 in Liverpool. He was sixty-two years old and due to his frailty, his head was almost torn off as his body dropped through the trapdoor.

Reservoirs have also been the place of demise for many a victim. Before a dam was built and the valley flooded above Glasgow to supply the city, there was a farmhouse known as Hoolet House in which a wealthy but grumpy middle-aged farmer named Hector McKinnon lived. For many years there was no laughter at the farm and at night just one light from a candle shone.

That was until the farmer returned home following a visit to Falkirk with a young bride, Mary. After that Hoolet House was a different place – there was laughter and light. People began to visit and were made most welcome by the couple, who threw lavish parties that propelled them into the high-society circles of the area. But then, just as suddenly, the farmer returned to his old miserly ways and closed the farm to visitors. All but one of the servants, a young Irishman, left the house saying the farmer had become irascible, beat them and often did not pay them for the work they had done. They were worried about his young wife, who he beat and treated like an animal, and she was the reason the young Irishman stayed at the farm despite constant beatings from Hector.

One day Hector went to market, little knowing that his wife and the Irishman were planning to run away together. Upon his return much shouting and screaming was heard coming from the farmhouse but no one dared to venture up to see what was going on. Hector was seen in the village later that day ashen white and with cuts to his face and hands. He said later that he discovered Mary and Thomas getting ready to run away with all his money, about £200, which he tried to wrestle off them but lost the fight, claiming he was knocked unconscious. He organised a search party the next day and for several days after that, explaining he wanted his wife and money back. As the days progressed the couple could not be found. As the months went by people claimed to have seen Thomas and Mary around the house but upon approach they would disappear into the night. The sightings were so vivid that the local magistrate visited to search the house in case Hector was keeping them captive, given his nasty character. At the same time, the animals on the farm began to die of a mystery illness and the farmer had to bury them. He employed men to help him when his farm horse died but became agitated when they started to dig near a large tree. Too late – a hand was found, and then the mangled remains of the farmer's wife and the Irishman were discovered. The young couple had been slashed to ribbons of flesh and bones by a billhook found in the grave with them, buried alongside the few belongings they had in a small cloth bag, including a pair of dance shoes and a beautiful dress which was also slashed. On seeing the faces of the labourers, who now realised what he had done, Hector turned on his heels and, as if on a pre-planned escape, rode off on his riding horse with his money and some goods, never to be seen again. After some time of absence, the farmland was divided amongst the nearby farms and the house fell into ruin before the waters covered it forever.

A supply of clean water has always been a concern for growing cities and the reservoir at Battersea was built for that purpose. Silas Barlow was found guilty of the double murder of his former sweetheart Ellen Soper, who was twenty-seven, and their young child, at Battersea on 11 September 1876. They had lived together and she had left him to move to lodgings to free herself of his controlling nature. He visited her twice at the new address, bringing cakes for her each time and she always felt sick after he left. Within a few weeks she died and the next day Barlow collected the child, saying that a cousin would look after the child. The landlady had her doubts and went off to follow Barlow. She lost sight of him in the alleyways but later, as she walked to fetch beer for her husband, found the body floating in Battersea reservoir. The body was identified and, when examined, was found to contain the poison strychnine. Barlow was arrested and charged with murder after searches of his home produced bottles of poison – the same poison that had killed Soper. Barlow denied killing the woman but later admitted that he had killed the child. The sentence of death was carried out by William Marwood in London on 19 December 1876.

Many deaths go unsolved either because water has removed vital evidence or decomposition is such that the body cannot be identified. On Sunday 25 March 1877 the body of William Saunders, a thirty-four-year-old gas company labourer, was found kicked to death and thrown into a pond near Penge cricket club in London. As the police investigated they discovered he had been drinking the previous evening with next-door neighbours until about 9p.m. Returning home for more cash, his forty-five-year-old wife gave him a shilling to continue his drinking. Around ten o'clock he was seen quarrelling with his lodger, James Dempsey, who was engaged to Saunders' stepdaughter, Jane Inman. When Mrs Saunders' elder son, Alfred Inman, and Dempsey were interviewed by the police their statements didn't match as they both claimed that they had been in all day but had forgotten that Dempsey had gone out briefly to buy whisky. The witness who had seen Saunders quarrelling with Dempsey was visited by Dempsey and then retracted her statement, saying that she wasn't sure now whether she had seen the quarrel or whether she had seen two other people fighting. All this convinced the police that Dempsey was guilty, but with the only witness refusing to help they were forced to let the case drop.

Love and murder have an unfortunate way of blending when things go wrong and one party does not accept the end of a relationship. On 28 February 1928 Harold Merry married Florence at Bromsgrove registrar's office. They had a happy marriage but by 1942 they had five children ranging from one to fourteen years old, and money and time were tight. Later on in 1942, Joyce Dixon appeared on the scene at the factory and she soon became Harold's lover. Dixon, despite a mental illness, had kept a job as a shorthand typist at Austin Aero works in Birmingham, where she met Merry who was working at the same factory as aircraft inspector. The couple got on well and Dixon had been told by Merry that he was a single man even though he never obtained a divorce from his wife. It was not until they had been going out for weeks that Merry confessed that he was a married man, but by this time Dixon had fallen in love with him and chose to ignore the fact that he was married. In September 1941, Dixon had a week's holiday planned but, unable to get hold of Merry, she sent him a letter to his home in Redditch. Written in a strange hand, Florence Merry opened it and was so upset by what she read that she had nothing more to do with her husband. The following Sunday he went to his sister's but when he returned he found that he was locked out of his home and Florence refused to allow him back. Merry, who was upset by his wife's actions, chose to return to stay at his sister's house. He continued to live with his sister until 19 March 1944, when he returned home to live with Florence again after much pleading for forgiveness.

It was common knowledge in the factory that Merry and Dixon were a couple. When Merry suggested that he and Dixon have a weekend away to have some quiet time, Dixon readily agreed, especially when Merry added that he thought they should get engaged. Merry had to do the proper thing first and speak to Dixon's mother to gain permission to go away, but she did not approve of her unmarried daughter going to London and sharing a hotel room with a man. However, news of the engagement helped and she finally agreed. Dixon didn't realise that Merry needed a hotel receipt to show he had booked in with another woman and thus obtain a divorce from his wife, leaving him free to marry her. On Saturday 21 March 1942 they went to a hotel in London where they decided to stay until the 27th. The receipt was obtained on a letterhead from a sister hotel but it was enough to get a divorce. Joyce Dixon went home to a grilling as her mother had been contacted by a supervisor and told her that her daughter had gone off with a married man; they had a bitter row and she stormed out. Dixon carried on meeting Merry where she could, usually at railway stations, where they spent time travelling from New Street Birmingham to Walsall and Wolverhampton before returning.

Early on 30 March one of Dixon's younger brothers, Norman, telephoned their older brother, Victor, to tell him that their sister had not come home. They went to her place of work and were told that neither she nor Merry had come in that day. They then went round to Merry's house where the door was opened by Florence. They explained the problem and asked to speak to Merry but just as Florence shouted upstairs for her husband a strange gurgling noise was heard from the bedroom. They rushed upstairs to find Merry with an electric flex around his neck trying desperately to choke himself. They tore the flex from his neck and the brothers demanded to know what he had done with their sister. To Victor and Norman's horror, Merry then confessed that he had killed her. They took him into Redditch police station where he repeated the claim to Sergeant Albert Morris. Merry admitted he'd strangled and drowned Joyce Dixon in the pool in fields at the back of her house. In the afternoon he took the police and Victor Dixon to a pond where her body was floating face down. Merry was taken back to the police station to be charged with murder. During a search a notebook was found and on one page was written 'goodbye to all, we are terribly in love with each other'. They also found a piece of paper on which he had written:

> Joyce and myself have been living as man and wife, hoping I should be able to get a divorce from my wife. We found it impossible to carry on, so we decided to die together. For God's sake forgive her; she is so happy now she knows we are going to die together.

The note was signed by them both.

On 31 March Merry first appeared at a police court, which was adjourned until 2 April. On 23 April and for the next two days Merry appeared in court and was formally charged with the murder of Joyce Dixon. His trial opened in Birmingham on 17 July 1942 under Mr Justice Croom-Johnson. The trial lasted just two days. The most damning piece of evidence was Merry's own statement to the police. When Dixon had told him that after all that had happened she feared her mother was losing her love for her, she had been very upset and said that they could no longer go on. She was in tears when she said that they could not get married now, and it would be better if they died together. At this point Merry wrote the suicide note and they both signed it. The two lovers walked from Broad Street and then took a tram back to where Joyce Dixon lived. They talked for about an hour outside her lodgings and decided that they should carry out the suicide plan. This is when they started the walk across the fields, where, according to his statement, Merry said: 'I will kill you first and promise you faithfully I will die with you.' Near the pond was a stile over the fence. This is where Merry took off his necktie and tried to strangle Dixon. After some time she collapsed and there was blood coming from her mouth. He then pushed her through the railings to the other side of the fence. She was still conscious and kept groaning, 'I love you.' He said he must have blacked out at this time and did not remember anything else, just coming out of the pond and seeing Dixon floating face down in it. Twice he tried to kill himself using his own necktie, but as he fell almost unconscious into the cold water the shock of it revived him. He spent the whole night standing in the cold water and it was not until early morning that he left to go home. His wife was annoyed at him coming in at 7.10a.m., soaking wet. He claimed he'd fallen into the brook before going upstairs to have a bath and rest.

Just before his trial Merry had withdrawn his statement, claiming that the first part was true – that they had made a suicide pact and that he had tried to strangle Joyce Dixon but because it hadn't worked he decided to leave. He called her to come out of the pond. She didn't, but he walked on for a number of minutes. Realising she had not caught up with him, he went back only to find her face down the pond. The pond, known as Turves Green, showed signs of a struggle near the stile that Merry had referred to and drag marks from the stile to the edge of the pond. The post-mortem performed on the body stated there was a large amount of chickweed and mud all over it and the red ligature mark around Dixon's neck was broader on the left side where the ligature might have crossed. The ultimate cause of death was by drowning but she had first been brought to near death by strangulation. The jury returned a verdict of guilty and Merry was sentenced to death.

An appeal was launched on 26 August before Justices Humphreys, Hilbery and Tucker, where the defence put forward three main grounds. Considering all points, the judges ruled there had been no misdirection so the appeal was lost. On the morning of Thursday 10 September 1942 Harold Oswald Merry was executed by Thomas Pierrepoint, assisted by Henry Critchell, at Birmingham.

A case that was to outrage a community was that of Henry Gaskin. In 1913 Henry Thomas Gaskin, who was then just twenty-one years old, married Elizabeth Talbot, who then lived at Hednesford, Staffordshire.

A child was soon born to the couple but in March 1914 Gaskin went to prison for theft after losing his job and finding money was difficult. He was released from Portland Prison on the Isle of Wight in early 1916 and Gaskin joined up to fight in the trenches of France. He did not return to England until September 1917, for a week, only to find that while he had been away his wife had given birth to two further children with two different men. During this time they lived with Elizabeth's mother, Emily Talbot, and appeared happy to the outside world. He returned to the front and was finally demobbed in early 1919. On 6 January 1919, given that Gaskin was still away when conception happened, she gave birth to her fourth child. On his return he decided that he would not go back to Emily Talbot's home and instead would stay with his mother Harriet. On Wednesday afternoon, 19 February 1919, a friend of Gaskin's, Tom Saunders, visited Emily Talbot with a note for Elizabeth. It read: 'Meet me round the pool at once important.' It was not signed so Tom explained it was written by Gaskin.

As Elizabeth had not returned that night, by the next day Emily Talbot had grown somewhat concerned and went to see Gaskin at his mother's house. Gaskin denied meeting Elizabeth the previous day, to which Emily replied that he sent a note with Tom Saunders asking for a meeting. Faced with this, Gaskin admitted that he had arranged to meet Elizabeth because he wanted to discuss the possibility of divorce, but after thinking it over he decided it might be best if he didn't. He did not keep the appointment and had no idea what had happened to his wife. Emily Talbot was suspicious and so reported him to the police. As a result of what she told him Inspector George Woolley went to West Cannock Colliery on 20 February to interview Gaskin where he worked. Gaskin admitted sending the note to Elizabeth and also said that he had decided not to meet up with her because he felt it was not the right time. The inspector then walked around the village and, on talking to a number of people, was told that they had seen Gaskin with Elizabeth on the road leading to the valley pit. Gaskin explained that the witnesses must be mistaken because he was in the public house at 2p.m. and home by 3p.m., and that night he had gone out to a cinema. However, the inspector spoke to the witnesses again and believed that Gaskin was not telling the whole truth. On the afternoon of the 21st, as Gaskin went to clock on at work, he found Supt John Morrey and Woolley waiting to take him to the police station. At the police station Gaskin was cautioned and held in custody while investigations continued into the evening. The inspector visited Gaskin's home and took possession of his clothing, both washed and unwashed. On the 22nd, Emily Talbot contacted the police because she had received a letter from Elizabeth, postmarked Birmingham, which had been posted at 12.05p.m. on Friday 21 February. In the letter it said:

Mrs Talbot,

Lizzie is quite all right she is with me now. I met her at Hednesford on Thursday. She was crying, and she told me that the husband was making a fool of her so I told her to leave all and come with me. She will send you some money when we get to London. She will write herself when we get there and she's very upset now. I can assure you she will be alright with me. Hoping you don't mind. From Lizzies friend W. Brooks.

Emily Talbot could not remember a friend called Brooks and thought that the letter had been sent by Gaskin to cover up whatever he had done to her daughter. Gaskin was confronted with the letter but demanded that he be returned to his cell, which he was allowed to do. Some time later he called the sergeant who was on duty asking to talk to the inspector. Supt Morrey was available and Gaskin announced that he wanted to show him where the body was. Gaskin rode in a taxi and directed them to Victoria Street, where he stopped the vehicle at the gasworks and said 'over there'. He then took the police to a large gas holder surrounded by a tank of water. He pointed down into the dark mix of water and oil, saying that her body was in the water; he intimated that he would now take them to where he committed the deed. Getting back into the cab, Gaskin took the police to a corner of a wood near the offices of Cannock and Rugeley mining company and pointed out an area under the trees of dried blood and remains of clothing. At the police station he made a statement which read:

I, Henry Thomas Gaskin, being of a sober and sound state of mind, do make this statement of my own free will and without any fear or favour. On Wednesday the 19th of February, 1919, I met my wife by arrangement on the Rugeley Road at 2:20p.m. and proceeded with her to the woods by the Cannock and Rugeley Colliery. She wanted to know why I would come home and there's nobody there only mother and dad. I asked her to come into the woods where we will talk things over in. I said what do you mean by having those bastard kids while I was away? I know you went to Yorkshire

with Sgt Walker then to Birmingham and then to London. She said it was my
fault and I should have come home instead of going off into the Army. Then I
wanted to know who the last kids father was and she said it is Monty's.

As the statement went on, it explained that she wanted to go to bed with
him, at which point he broke and said, 'how dare you want to bed me
after what you've done'. She struggled free but Gaskin grabbed her again,
thumped her and told her she was going to hell where she belonged. He
took her deeper into the wood, holding her hand, when suddenly he
dragged her by the hair some yards further into the wood, then stood over
her for about a minute. When she attempted to get up he pushed her down
again, saying, 'I have not done with you yet'. He then hit her with his fist
in her left ear, saying, 'That's for Sgt Walker,' and hit her in the right, saying,
'That is for Monty'; then he struck her in the right eye, saying, 'That is for
whoring in Birmingham,' and in the left, saying, 'That is for the whoring
in London.' Gaskin then rolled up his sleeve, saying, 'Now I'll tear you
inside out and show it to you.' Then he forced his hand and arm into her
womb, up to his elbow, but failing to draw anything out, made about four
snowballs and forced them inside her, saying, 'These will cool you down a
bit, you bitch.' Semi-conscious, Elizabeth began to kick and make noises
from her throat. Shouting at her that he was going to stop that row, he broke
off a large twig from a tree and forced it down her throat, saying 'Chew that
if you like.' He then took his knife and cut all her clothing off and while
he was hiding her hat and shoes she got up into a kneeling position. When
he returned to continue the attack, she murmured 'Harry' and raised her
arms up level with the shoulders. He knelt down in front of her and said,
'Do you see me?' She shook her head, which he took to mean yes. He then
asked if she could hear him and she nodded, to which he said, 'listen to me;
I am going to kill you and cut you to pieces'. He then kicked her under the
chin and she rolled over; he cut her open from womb to navel, caught her
by the heels and bent her up, causing some of the entrails to pour out of
her stomach cavity. She did not speak but put her hands over the large cut,
trying to put her lower intestine back into her body. Gaskin then stood up
and put his right heel on her neck until she finished struggling; then he cut
her up to the neck and pulled out the rest of her intestines before he trailed
them around her, damning her to hell as he attacked her genitals with a
knife. She was still breathing when he covered her up with her own clothes
and left her where she lay to die a painful and lonely death. He reached

home about 5.30p.m., washed, changed and went to the cinema. After being in the cinema for half an hour he made an excuse to leave the building and proceeded to Hednesford by bus. He went into the woods where the body lay, dragged it to the edge of the wood, cut off the head and almost cut the left leg off too. Then he dragged the body to the gasometer nearby and threw the head into the water surrounding it. He carried the body to the same place and, after forcing a 2in gas pipe down into the torso to weight it down, he threw it into the water where he had led the police.

Gaskin finished his gruesome statement at 2.30a.m. and was charged with murder. Armed with the knowledge of where to find Elizabeth Gaskin's body, police officers with grappling hooks began to drag the waters round the gas meter. Sgt Thomas John Heath found the headless body, and on the same day Gaskin had been charged. Elizabeth had indeed been horribly mutilated in the manner the killer had described. The search continued but it was not until 25 February that the battered head was discovered. A post-mortem was carried out by Dr John Potter, who eventually catalogued her serious injuries. Although not fully reported in newspapers, this murder earned Gaskin the name the Hednesford Ripper. The confession that Gaskin made was so horrific that at the inquest of the dead woman all females were asked to leave the court before the document was read out. A verdict of wilful murder was returned and after a number of appearances Gaskin was sent to trial. Gaskin's case came before Justice Roche at Stafford on 4 July 1919. Gaskin had put forward defence that he was insane at the time of the crime due to his wife's infidelity.

To help the police case against Gaskin, a number of witnesses were interviewed and they all reported that, on the day, Gaskin seemed as if he hadn't a care in the world. He chatted away to a number of people, including John Thomas Gary and his friend Tom Saunders who delivered the note from the pub. Gary said that at 1p.m. he and Gaskin were in the Uxbridge Hotel together, but by 1.40p.m. they had moved to the Plough and Harrow, where they stayed until 2p.m. At that time Gary went back towards his own house while Gaskin headed off towards the old pool in the woods. A number of witnesses reported seeing Gaskin with Elizabeth on their way to the woods or in the woods themselves. A man working in the Cannock and Rugeley colliery office, Thomas Barton, said on 19 February he was in the boardroom and he saw Gaskin and Elizabeth walk along the edge of the plantation where, at one stage, the couple parted, Gaskin going on into the woods and Elizabeth walking along the hedge line. He lost sight of Elizabeth as she walked over the hill. Another witness, Miss Sarah Southall, saw Gaskin and his wife walking at the side of plantation at around 3p.m. or perhaps a little earlier. Another witness swore that when he was on leave in 1917 Gaskin threatened to shoot his wife and even produced a gun. Even the use of a wheelbarrow to take Elizabeth's body to where he was trying to hide it left conspicuous tracks in the snow. James Bradbury, a miner, testified that at 11.50p.m. on 19 February he found a wheelbarrow in the middle of the road close by the plantation.

Dr John Potter gave evidence that a rusty section of iron piping, 1in in diameter and just over 6ft long, had been pushed through the chest part of Elizabeth's headless torso. It was at a slanting position and passed through the belly towards the left side of her body. The pipe extended 3ft 4in from the opening of the neck. He commented that there were many minor cuts on the body but among the more serious ones was one opened on the front part of the chest from the neck, down to the breast bone. The cut in the belly was between 10in and 4in wide; the left elbow was broken and Elizabeth's vagina, womb and labium had been cut away on the left side and were missing, as was the bladder. The head had been severed between the fourth and fifth vertebrae and when it was recovered the total height of the body could be determined at 5ft 2in. The cause of the slow death was shock and loss of blood from extensive wounds. The prosecution then showed that Gaskin had paid a stranger 2s 6d to write the Brooks letter in order to hide his tracks and carefully disposed of the body.

His defence team now called a number of witnesses to describe that Gaskin's behaviour was far from normal in order to get a plea of 'insane'. An army colleague who had served with Gaskin in the Engineers' Tunnelling Company said that one day, close to the German lines, they'd been digging a tunnel when it was blown up. Gaskin was buried in the tunnel and it took hours to get him out. After that Gaskin started to behave strangely and would start to shake whenever there was heavy shellfire. It was also noted that whilst he shook he also had no sense of danger and no fear of being killed. Since his return from the trenches on 4 January 1919 Gaskin's behaviour had become even stranger. He rarely drank but when he did he became erratic and more aggressive.

The jury retired at 4.28p.m. to consider their verdict and returned at 4.52p.m. A verdict of guilty of murder was given so the judge sentenced him to death. Gaskin muttered that he did not intend to kill her, just teach her a lesson. Gaskin appealed on 21 July 1919 on the grounds that he was insane and that his former wife's conduct had been such that he had been sorely provoked. Giving his judgement, Lord Isaacs said it was plain that the crime was premeditated and this was the behaviour of a sane man. Although some 6,000 people signed a petition for the reprieve, the execution was carried out. At 8a.m. on Friday 8 August 1919, Henry Thomas Gaskin was hanged at Birmingham by John Ellis and William Willis. A small crowd had gathered to read the notices of the execution posted outside the prison.

Murder for financial gain is the most common kind, and a number of such crimes have occurred in very beautiful locations. Around the area of Loch Assynt one hears many stories, including the sad tale of a pedlar, Murdoch Grant, who was murdered as he travelled around the paths, trading goods and lending money. It was known that Murdoch carried all his cash on him as he distrusted banks and his home was often broken into when he was on the road. On the morning of 11 March 1830 he was last seen alive as he set off to sell his wares at a wedding in Assynt. He never arrived. A month later, his body was discovered floating in the loch by a courting couple. Murdoch Grant's body, with a large gash to the back of the head, was removed from the loch and laid in a coffin. The local custom whenever there was a murder was for the residents of Assynt to press their forefinger on the forehead of the victim to prove they were not the killer. This tradition is known as 'touch-proof' as it was believed that a guilty person would bleed from the finger on contact with the corpse. Only one person refused to do this, saying he was an educated man who did not believe in such rubbish, the local schoolmaster, Macleod. Suspicion immediately fell on him, supported by the fact that he was known to be in debt and had a reputation for buying women's favours and living beyond his means. There was no proof that the money he had suddenly come by was from a distant aunt who he said had passed away, leaving him an inheritance, which he had collected from a solicitor. When pressed he could not remember which solicitor he had visited, or where, so while the police had no further proof, they were not convinced by his story. However, Macleod did not get away with his crime. What he did not count on was Kenneth Frazer, a local man with the gift of second sight who had helped many people over the years and so was a trusted member of the community. Frazer walked into the magistrate's house and told an astounded audience of how Macleod had met Murdoch and tried to extend a loan. Murdoch refused. Macleod hit him on the head then stole the rucksack, took the money and some of the goods, before hiding it in a nearby hollowed out tree. The police were contacted and searched the area where Frazer claimed the rucksack had been hidden. It was soon found, along with a jacket known to have belonged to Macleod, stuffed into the rucksack. That would explain why he was wearing a new oilcloth coat he claimed to have bought, which turned out to have belonged to Grant, giving more damning evidence the police needed. Macleod was arrested for murder as he took a class at the school and he quickly confessed. His trial was swift and Macleod was sentenced to the gallows and his body was left hanging in chains for years.

 Sometimes murder arises out of something as simple as fellow workers not getting on. When Father James' thirty-six-year-old housekeeper, Mary Callan, went missing on 16 May 1927, chauffeur Gerard Toal expressed no concern. He had not got on with Callan, who had been appointed as housekeeper to run the house for the priest. It was thought that Callan had gone to visit her mother but the old lady said she had not seen her for months. Chauffeur Toal claimed she had left the house after giving him dinner and taking a cake out of the oven with instructions to place it in the tin when it had cooled down. For weeks her position was kept open but in the end a new housekeeper had to be hired. The new housekeeper had been tidying up the rooms and noticed a number of bicycle parts in Toal's room. When asked by the priest where he got them from he admitted they were stolen. The following April, because Toal was a very lazy chauffeur and didn't keep the car or priest's bicycle clean, he was sacked. There was a huge row and Toal said that he was going to Canada. Ten days later, however, the priest was called to Dundalk where the police had arrested Toal for theft. They were also suspicious because whilst in the cell Toal boasted to a fellow inmate that he'd done away with Callan. To try to help him get a reduced charge, the cellmate told the police what Toal had said and they decided to go to the priest's house and gardens. After a few hours searching, they found women's clothing, more bicycle parts burnt in an ash pit near an old quarry, and eventually the body of Mary Callan, weighted down and decomposing in an abandoned water-filled quarry. When Police Inspector McKeown and his officers confronted Toal, he broke down and confessed that there had been a terrible row between the two of them in May 1927. He swore her death was an accident, saying that he pushed her and she hit her head on the cooking range as she fell and never woke up. At the trial the judge advised the jury against bringing a verdict of manslaughter and on 28 August 1928 at Dublin Jail he was hanged.

In Essex, in 1899, a murder took place that followed years of deceit and planning at Moat Farm. Samuel Herbert Dougal was a big man at over 6ft tall and weighing in at 16 stone, with a neatly trimmed beard and an air of simmering wildness about him developed during his twenty-one years in the army. His charisma was infectious to many of the women he met. When he was fifty-two he met Camille Holland, but at the time was married to his third wife after having lost the first two in highly suspicious circumstances whilst he was serving in the army, with rumours of poisoning circulating around him. He had been the suspect in each case but nothing was ever proven, partly due to the fact that they had died whilst he was away on duty. He left the Royal Engineers in 1877 with the rank of quartermaster sergeant, worked at a number of jobs until sailing to Dublin, where he met and married Sarah White in 1892. He divided his time between England and Ireland until 1895, then he started work as a hospital messenger in Dublin. He was dismissed from that job for dishonesty and moved to England, where he was also dismissed, arrested and tsentenced to twelve months' hard labour for theft. His attempt to commit suicide before arriving at Pentonville resulted in him being committed to an asylum to serve out the remainder of his sentence. He was, by all accounts, a ladies' man, married with three children, yet he had a number of affairs in which he would seduce ladies and then steal from them before disappearing.

When he met Camille Holland all he saw was a pretty spinster with a lot of money. She had inherited £6,000 in 1893 in the form of cash, stocks and shares, and jewellery from an aunt. It gave her an allowance to stay in hotels and boarding houses, where she occasionally wrote to nephews. The couple first met at an Earl's Court exhibition in 1898, when Miss Holland was staying at a Bayswater boarding house. She was visited there by Captain Dougal, as he now called himself. At this time soldiers and ex-soldiers were revered by the public and Dougal was quick to take advantage of the situation. Camille quickly fell for the engaging captain and Dougal must have believed that he had struck gold. Unfortunately, Miss Holland misled him into thinking she was better off than she was. Something worried her and so she finished the affair. Dougal, not wishing to give up on the money, pursued Miss Holland, who was soon back in his grasp. They spent a little time together in Sussex and Dougal found that Miss Holland was not as generous as he expected and so he suggested they buy a farm. After viewing several properties they eventually entered into negotiations to buy Moat Farm (Coldhams Farm) in Essex. A fortnight later the couple left Sussex to lodge at an address in Saffron Walden prior to moving into Moat Farm. They moved into the farm on 27 April 1899. Dougal had chosen the farm well, set deep in Essex countryside, isolated, surrounded by trees, with no close neighbours. The feature was a moat that completely surrounded the property, panned by a single narrow bridge to give access to the house. Later and under oath, Dougal said it was the place 'I wanted, and I thought the moat would be very useful, because after the farm had been transferred to me I thought it might be easy for the lady to be found in the moat'. Two days after their arrival Dougal and Miss Holland were joined by a servant girl, Lydia Faithfull, who was soon replaced by Florence Havies.

Dougal now had Florence in his sights, not for money but simply because she was an attractive younger woman. On the first morning after arriving Dougal crept up behind Florence in the kitchen, grabbed her around the waist and started to kiss her neck. Florence strongly objected, and she complained to Camille, who had difficulty in persuading her to stay. Undeterred, Dougal entered her bedroom whereupon she screamed and Miss Holland soon arrived on the scene to see Dougal vanish down a stairwell to the kitchen. Florence spent two nights sleeping in the same room as Miss Holland to avoid his unwelcome attentions and at the end of the unhappy week things seemed to have settled down a little. Dougal and Camille went out on Friday 19 May in the pony trap. That was the last time anyone saw Camille Holland alive. Dougal decided it was time to get rid of Camille because he wanted the money. His plan originally was to dump the body in the moat to make it look like accidental drowning after a fall from the small bridge. Upon reflection he realised that there would be an inquest and things would point to him, so he decided that he would shoot her and dump her body in a drainage ditch, hoping the mud and water would conceal what he'd done.

In his later confession he said:

I had pushed the trap into the coach house and I could see by the light at the back of the house that the servant girl was still there doing her work. I stepped up on the side of the trap, reached down for the revolver I had previously hidden in the barn, and as Miss Holland stood near the back door looking at the moon I shot her. I wasn't standing very far from her, and of course I was a little higher, because I was still on the step of the trap. She dropped like a log, and then I pulled her body into the coach house.

Dougal then spent the rest of the night disposing of the body. On five occasions he returned to the farmhouse, the first to tell Florence that her mistress had suddenly gone to London. Knowing that she was on her own with this horrible man, she was so terrified that she put furniture against her bedroom door and sat up all night by the window fully clothed waiting for the sunrise. The next day he told Florence that he had received a letter from Miss Holland that morning saying she was going to have a little holiday. But Florence was still terrified at the thought of being alone with Dougal and she screamed with relief when her mother arrived to pick her up. Soon afterwards his wife, Sarah, and daughter arrived at the farm. Dougal explained that Miss Holland was financing the purchase of a farm and had left on a health cruise. To the few neighbours he explained his wife's presence by introducing her as his daughter and his daughter as a granddaughter. He then set about forging Miss Holland's signature, soon drawing upon her assets.

With cash withdrawals, sale of holdings and transfer into his name of Moat Farm providing him with the funds needed to slip easily into the role of benevolent country landowner, Dougal lived contented. He even subscribed towards the clock at Clavering church. For almost four years he enjoyed the fruits of his labours on that May night in 1899 when he murdered Camille Holland. There were a number of servant girls who worked at the farm in that time, many of whom stayed for a short while, not prepared to put up with his constant sexual harassment. Rumours started in the surrounding villages that Dougal liked to pay young women to undress and cycle about his field naked in front of him before he seduced them. This was confirmed when a labourer, cutting across fields to the village, was nearly knocked over by a local girl completely naked riding a bicycle in the field, egged on by a similarly naked Dougal. Quarrels began between Dougal and his wife, who was not happy about all the young women being hired and interfered with by her husband. She eventually left with a farm labourer in 1902.

Eighteen-year-old servant girl Kate Cranwell had arrived a month prior to Sarah's departure. When Kate left three months later she was pregnant and soon started proceedings against Dougal for childcare. Another local girl arrived at the farm as a servant and also left two months later; she too was pregnant. People had begun to wonder where Miss Holland had gone, given the fact that four years ago she left for a short cruise. Locals expressed their suspicions openly and PC James Drew wrote to his chief constable concerning his fear that Miss Holland had been murdered and buried somewhere on the farm. When further enquiries were made at the banks, stockbrokers and solicitors, they suddenly realised that all the signatures from May 1899 were forgeries. Superintendent Charles Pryke decided to visit Dougal in order to find out where Miss Holland was. Dougal denied all knowledge of her whereabouts, saying that they'd had a little tiff and she said she would never want to see him again and had left with her bags. The tiff was about Florence, who claimed he had tried to get into bed with her which he said was not true. He denied all knowledge of shares or stocks and at the end of the conversation Superintendent Charles Pryke was initially convinced that Dougal was telling the truth.

The visit by Superintendent Pryke sent Dougal into a panic and he withdrew over £600 from two accounts and then left the farm. On Friday 13 March he stayed overnight in London to meet the pregnant servant girl who succeeded Kate Cranwell. They travelled to Bournemouth where they spent a long weekend at a hotel then the following Tuesday the girl returned to the farm, leaving Dougal in London. He walked to the Bank of England and tried to change the £10 notes he had drawn out the week before, the serial numbers of which had been circulated as having been fraudulently obtained. The police were called and when they arrived Dougal tried to run off but was quickly caught. At Cloak Lane police station he was charged for forging Camilla Holland's name on the cheque the previous August and for obtaining a sum of £28 5s. Two days later, on Thursday 19 March, he appeared before the magistrates at Saffron Walden charged with cheque forgery.

Over the next six weeks he was remanded in custody as more evidence came forward about financial affairs and transactions that were forged in the name of Camille Holland. The police were given a warrant to search Moat Farm and soon uncovered clothing and items belonging to the missing woman, items that certainly wouldn't be left behind if she had planned to leave. They first searched the moat as being the obvious place to hide a body; then they turned their attentions to the land around the farm. A labourer who had filled in the drainage ditch came forward and took the police to the line of the once water-filled ditch which he had been asked to fill in by Dougal. On Monday 27 April a constable discovered a ladies' button boot containing the remains of a foot. Careful excavation revealed what remained of Camille Holland. The landlady the couple had stayed with in Saffron Walden had identified some of the clothing that was on the body. An inquest opened two days later in a barn on the farm. Florence was called as a witness and she described all the things that Dougal used to do, like the time he put his arm around her waist and tried to kiss her. She went on to describe how he got into her room two nights later where, in rude undertones, he had tried to get into her bed and seduce her. She then described how and when she had last seen Miss Holland alive on 19 May 1899. Dr Augustus Joseph Pepper, of St Mary's Hospital, London, carried out the post-mortem on the remains of Miss Holland at the farm. He discovered a bullet inside the skull and explained that the bullet entered the right side and was stopped on the left and rested in the brain. The bullet wounds could not have been self-inflicted. The position of the woman indicated that the shot had been fired from behind as the direction of the bullet was from above, down and to the left. The coroner spoke to the jury and said: 'If satisfied with the evidence, I think you can safely say that it is your duty to return a verdict of wilful murder against Dougal.'

The jury agreed that he was guilty of murder yet Dougal maintained he was an innocent man. After the inquest into Miss Holland's death it was given that her death was not suicide but murder. Dougal was committed to trial at the Chelmsford Assizes on 22 June 1903. Prior to that Dougal had written to all his lovers asking them to attend the trial. The trail started shakily when Mrs Pollock, the former landlady, failed initially to identify Dougal. The jury heard that Miss Holland and Dougal had been getting on well before she disappeared. Other evidence in the case included a firearms expert and the police officer who found the cartridges and pistol used in the murder at the farm. Kate Cranwell gave evidence about the way she was treated and said she had seen the pistol in the kitchen. She had also been asked to pack up a trunk of Miss Holland's clothing thinking it was being sent on to her. The trial took just two days and the jury an hour and a quarter to reach the decision that Dougal was guilty of the murder of Miss Holland. He remained unemotional when the sentence of death was passed. His defence went to appeal but it was dismissed. Before his execution he claimed the death was an accident and that he had panicked when he realised she was dead. Dougal was executed at 8a.m. on Tuesday 14 July 1903. Before he died he was asked by the Revd Blackmore whether he was guilty or not guilty of the murder. He replied 'guilty' as he fell to his death.

After murder there is often a prime suspect and only time is needed to pull together the evidence required to convict the murderer. But when the suspect is known, yet all the available evidence is hearsay, and the case is dismissed, where can the relative of a victim go? On 26 May 1817, Mary Ashford, a housemaid, and bricklayer Abraham Thornton left a dance at the Three Tuns Inn, Castle Bromwich, just after midnight. At 6:30a.m. Mary's body was found in a water-filled pit. Bloodspots and footprints suggested that she had been chased by a man who assaulted her violently, raping her, and then chased her again to the pit where he drowned her. Abraham Thornton was the last person seen with Mary and so he was brought to the scene and it was found that his boots fitted the preserved footprints exactly, thus placing him at the scene. At his trial his counsel pointed out that the matching bootprint was made before the time of the struggle. Nobody had confirmed that Thornton had chased the girl and drowned her. He did not deny enjoying sexual intercourse with her, which he said was her desire as much as his. The rupture of her virgin hymen coupled with her menstrual flow caused the bloodspots and signs of blood on his clothing. The jury acquitted him. Mary's brother William, however, discovered a statute of Henry VII by which he could reopen proceedings with a private prosecution within a year and a day. He did so, only to be astonished when Thornton exploited the other half of the statute and threw a glove on the floor of the court while declaring not guilty, 'I am ready to defend the same with my body'. The same statute also said that he had the right to defend his word by combat and that William Ashford must fight him in combat to the death. If William won the fist fight, proving Thornton guilty, he would be hanged, and should Thornton win, he would be a free and innocent man. The private prosecution was hastily withdrawn as a consequence of this statement.

Having fled Australia on corruption charges in the 1920s, the former New South Wales Minister of Justice, Thomas Ley, set up home in London with his mistress Mrs Maggie Brook. Approaching sixty years of age, he became more and more paranoid that Maggie was having an affair with bartender John Mudie. In November 1947 he hired John Buckingham, a local businessman, to abduct Mudie and take him to his Knightsbridge home, where Ley and a builder, Smith, beat and strangled him. Mudie died pleading that he never had an affair with Maggie. The body was then taken to a chalk pit near Wolderingham where it was unceremoniously dumped. Buckingham turned King's evidence against Ley and Smith when he was arrested for murder and told how he was approached by Thomas Ley about taking Mudie to Ley's home and leaving him there with Smith. At the trial

Ley claimed that when he left Mudie in the cellar he was alive but bruised. The plan was to leave him there for a few hours to teach him a lesson and then let him go. He also claimed that when he went down to release Mudie he found that he was dead, strangled during his own efforts to escape. Both Ley and Smith denied murder. They were both condemned to death based on the evidence before the courts. A medical examination of Ley found him to be quite mad and he was transferred to Broadmoor to serve out the rest of his life. Smith too was reprieved the noose and his sentence was commuted to life imprisonment.

By the side of the main Gorleston to Beccles Road, the A143, is a deep pond known as Lily Pit, named after a woman who drowned there; it is located near Ottey's Farm. In 1888 a man named James Keable was riding home in the fog and fell into the pit and his body was only recovered a few days later when the fog lifted. The road itself used to be very uneven with sharp corners, one such corner next to the pit. In 1852 a mail coach carrying passengers careered off the road into the pit and only the driver survived to tell the tale. All six occupants and the horses perished, their bodies floating to the surface days later. A young farmhand from Ottey's Farm ran away with the only daughter of the farmer, Lily. The farmer and some of his friends had heard the rumours of the elopement and so waited by the side of the road in order to catch the couple. As the young man and his lover rode by, the farmer and the men jumped out, startling the horse. The daughter was thrown from the horse into the pit where, despite efforts to save her, she drowned. So upset was the farmer that he took off into the woods nearby and hanged himself.

'Witches' were often drowned in ponds and pools such as the one below Edinburgh Castle, where there was a manmade loch, Nor' Loch, that was part of the original castle's defence system. Over the years it went from a defence to a boating lake and later used for the ducking of those accused of being a witch. At the time they were being ducked the water was putrid from the polluted streams that carried animal and human waste to the loch. A woman accused of witchcraft would be stripped and strapped to a stool with thumbs and toes tied together before being ducked. If she drowned she was presumed innocent and would be seen as going to heaven. Should the 'witch' survive she would be taken to Castle Hill and burnt to death, with any remains thrown into the loch. By 1759, when the loch was drained to make way for new housing, a large number of bones and skulls were found in the mud at the bottom which were removed and buried outside the city.

One of the worst cases involving the murder of a 'witch' happened at Tring. In 1745 an elder of the village of Tring went to beg for milk from the local farmer, named Butterfield, as she was poor and her husband needed some sustenance. The farmer refused but heard Ruth Osborne muttering to herself that she hoped the devil would sweep in and carry off Butterfield's cattle. A few days later Butterfield fell ill and things on the farm went from good to bad, which he was convinced was due to the curse Osborne had placed on him. To help the farmer remove the curse, a white witch from Northamptonshire was asked to visit and place a counter-spell on him and his farm, as well as confirming that Osborne and her husband were witches. Six strong men with pitchforks were placed on guard outside the farmhouse, day and night, in order to keep any person or animal that may have been Osborne in disguise away from the farm. Charms were placed in the chimneys and at each entrance door to ward off evil. After a week Butterfield had taken a turn for the worst so the level of spell removal was increased. The white witch commanded that some thirty ale-drinking men were to be employed for the next stage, which was announced through town criers at Hemel Hempstead, Leighton Buzzard and Winslow on the market days to attract the highest number of people to help stage two. The message read out by the town criers was, 'This is to give notice that on

The practice of witch-ducking.

Monday next a man and woman are to be publicly ducked at Tring for their wicked crimes.'

Matthew Burton, an overseer from the poorhouse in Tring who had helped the couple over the years, heard news of the ducking so rushed to them and took the couple to what he thought was the safety of the workhouse. A mob had started to gather on the Sunday night so the master of the workhouse decided that they might be better off in the vestry of the parish church, where they hoped the sanctity would save them. On Monday the crowds had grown to a reported 5,000 people, which must have been a daunting spectacle for the villagers determined to save the couple from the ducking. The leader of the mob, on horseback and dressed in fine clothes, demanded the couple be put in front of him so that justice may be carried out. Matthew Burton tried to convince the mob that the couple were no longer in the building but the mob did not believe him and, knocking him to the floor with severe blows, ransacked the poorhouse looking for the couple and even the saltbox, where the cones of salt were stored, was searched in case the 'witches' were hiding in there. Finding no sign of the couple, they held Jonathan Tomkins, the master of the poorhouse, by the throat with threats that if the couple were not delivered to them he would be made to watch as the mob burnt the village to the ground. Under such pressures he gave the mob the location of the couple and fell to the ground on release praying to God for his forgiveness. The church door, although fortified with timbers, was smashed down and the couple were captured and dragged to Marlstone Green. There were several witnesses who testified at the inquest of the murder. John Holms said:

This man and woman were separately tied up in a cloth or sheet; then a rope was tied under the armpits of the deceased, and two men dragged her into a pond; and they dragged her sheer through the pond several times; and that Colley, having a stick in his hand, went into the pond, and turned the deceased up and down several times.

John Humphries also claimed:

Colley turned her over and over several times with a stick; that after the mob had ducked her several times, brought her to the shore and set by the pond side, and then dragged the old man in and ducked him; that after they had brought him to shore and set him by the pond side, they dragged the deceased in a second time; and that Colley went again into the pond, and turned and pushed the deceased about with a stick as before; and then she being brought to shore again, the man was also a second time dragged in, and underwent the same discipline as he had before; and being brought ashore , the deceased was a third time dragged into the pond; that Colley went into the pond again and took hold of the cloth or sheet in which she was wrapt, and pulled her up and down the pond till the same came from her, and then she appeared naked; that then Colley pushed her on the breast with his stick, which she endeavoured with her left hand to catch hold of, but he pulled it away, and that was the last time life was in her. When Colley came out of the pond, he went round among the people who were spectators of the tragedy, and collected money of them as a reward for the great pains he had taken in showing them sport in ducking the old witch, as he then called the deceased.

The case against Colley and twenty-one others who took part in the killings followed an inquest in which the death of Mrs Osborne was returned as murder. The case opened in July 1751, when Colley, William Humbles and Charles Young, alias Lee or Red Beard, were summoned for murder. During the evidence given against the men the pond was described as being just 2ft deep, with a deep layer of mud below the surface which meant the Osbornes could not sink. They heard that the mob had dragged the couple from the church, stripped them naked and tied their thumbs to the toes together before bundling them towards the pond where they were thrown in, trawled up and down the pond before thrown to the bank where members of the mob beat them with sticks, thumped and kicked them. Even after Ruth had died the mob continued to hit and kick her corpse. Eventually they became tired of kicking and so dragged the corpse of Ruth to the bed in which her husband, badly beaten, was being treated by the vicar. The mob pushed the reverend out of the way and tied Ruth's body to her husband, cheered and encouraged by Colley. The jury was so appalled at the way Ruth Osborne was treated that they found Thomas Colley guilty of murder. He was condemned to be executed on 22 August 1751. The night before the execution he spent at the St Albans Jail from where, at 5a.m. in a single carriage accompanied by his executioner with an escort of 108 men of the Horse Guards Blue with their officers and two trumpeters, they slowly travelled to his place of execution at Gubblecut cross. As his daughter and wife were talking to him a pistol shot rang out, causing the troops to react by aiming at windows of nearby houses where they feared an assassin was hiding. It turned out that a trooper, in the excitement of the moment, had discharged his pistol by mistake for which he was put on a charge. The Revd Randall of Tring administered Colley's last rites and read out a solemn declaration written by Colley:

> I beseech you all to take warning by an unhappy man's suffering; that you be not deluded into so absurd and wicked a conceit, as to believe that there are many such being upon earth as witches. It was a foolish and vein imagination, heightened and inflamed by the strength of liquor, which prompted me to be instrumental (with others as mad-brained as myself) in a horrid and barbarous murder of Ruth Osborne, the supposed witch, for which I am now so deservedly to suffer death. I am fully convinced of my former error, and with the sincerity of a dying man, declare that I do not believe there are such thing in being as a witch; and prey God that none of you, through a contrary persuasion, may hereafter be induced to think that you have the right in any shape to persecute, much less endanger the life of a fellow creature.
>
> I beg you all to pray to God to forgive me, and to wash clean my polluted soul in the blood of Jesus Christ, my saviour and redeemer.
>
> So exhorteth you all, the dying – Thomas Colley.

At 11a.m., after half an hour of praying and guarded by the troops, Colley was executed close to the spot he murdered Osborne and once dead his body was hung in chains from the same gallows. John Osborne, being much younger than his wife and a solidly built, strong man could not get work after the murder of his wife as the locals still feared that he could use his wizardry upon them and their livestock. Almost starving, with no home to go to as the mob had destroyed that by fire, he threw himself on the parish and ended his days in the Tring workhouse a broken man.

Misplaced paternal love has often led to murder, as we saw at Lily Pit, and the Broads are no different. As this area was being drained great tracts of land were taken by local people who wished to join the upper classes in land ownership. There developed great estates from the new land. A terrible man who ruled his household with a rod of steal took one of these large areas of land. When one of his daughters tried to run off with her true love the father followed. The eloping pair sailed off in a rowboat heading across Barton Broad when the boat was hit broadside with a large amount of shot from a punt-gun. The daughter was killed outright, her lover badly wounded. The boat was hauled ashore and the lover was told to leave –

which he did fearing he would be next to be shot. The father was filled with remorse when he realised he had killed his daughter. He made a vow to change his ways and begged the forgiveness of his dead daughter. His estate fell around him, his wife took his money and he died a poor, broken man.

At Thurlton, Norfolk, the area is renowned for the eerie spectacle of the Will-o'-the-Wisp or Jack o' Lanterns. These are caused by the release of methane gas that self-ignites, sometimes creating tall blue flames. Many a visitor or resident in the area has fallen for the misleading lights and perished in the cold waters of the nearby dykes. One such victim was Joseph Bexfield, a wherryman who knew of the ghostly lights, but on 11 August 1809, he must have followed them thinking they were people crossing the fields after a few pints in the pub. His body was discovered in a dyke with reed roots all around it. He is buried in the nearby church with his boots on, as was the tradition for sailors in the area.

4

CHILD MURDERS

Having lost his wife Bridget to a long illness in 1910 whilst living in a poor house in Linlithgow, Patrick Higgins had to take his two children, William and John, aged four and six, on the road to look for work. He had been discharged from active service in India due to his drinking and attacks of epilepsy. His drinking continued, and with three to feed the children often went hungry when their father drank their funds away. The family lived in woods, barns or wherever they could find shelter, often stealing potatoes and other vegetables from fields to live on. Eventually, a passer-by saw the state of the children Higgins had tried to hide away from public gaze and he was sent to prison for neglect whilst the boys went into another poor house where at least they were fed, cleaned and clothed. On his release Higgins collected the boys and put them into inns until the landlord threw them out for not paying bills. He tried to get the boys into various homes without success. On a stormy November night in 1911 Higgins tied his sons together with rope and attached them to a large slab of stone. Under the influence of alcohol, he threw the boys into the dark, cold waters of the Hopetoun Quarry to drown them before callously going off to drink more at the inn along the road. Over a year later the bodies of the boys, still tied together, floated to the surface where they were found by two farmhands who quickly called the police. Perhaps it was the cold water or some divine intervention, but the bodies were said to be as fresh as the day they went into the water. Identified as William and John Higgins, who their father claimed had found a home together, Patrick Higgins was soon dragged from the inn he had frequented after the murders by the police and an angry mob. At his trial he asked for mercy as he was at his wits' end and knew not what he was doing, in a drunken haze, until three days later, when he had a flashback to his crime. Until then in his mind he believed the boys were in a safe home together. Even though there was some public sympathy for Higgins, the judge felt his only option was to sentence him to death for the double murder of his sons. On 2 October 1913 Higgins was executed at Calton Jail, where a massive crowd had gathered in a sombre mood as they waited for the black flag to indicate that Higgins was dead. Because the boys' bodies were so well preserved they became a talking point with many medics and pathologists, the main reason for it being that most of the boys' fat had solidified into a soap-like substance in the cold water.

 A mother's love is said to know no bounds, except when the birth is unexpected, as happened to Elizabeth Harrard. She was unaware that she was pregnant so when she went into labour she thought she was dying. Her lover had long gone so she was on her own and working in the garden of the local workhouse, but had lived with a John Gadd as man and wife although they were not married. The child was large for the time, weighing in at 4lb and born a bastard. Because of the shame of a bastard child, Harrard was quick to hide the evidence of the birth and decided to smother the boy, wrap the body in newspaper and throw it that night into the river at Powder-Mills near Isleworth on 10 July. On Saturday 14 July the body was seen by farmer Mr Ions floating at the side of the river. He removed it and called for the local beadle, John Thackery, to collect the body. Thackery found the body had been taken out of the water and had a little grass and weed upon it. There was no swelling to the body yet a huge blow to the head was indicated by a plug of congealed blood. The hole was so huge that Thackery could place his finger inside and wiggle it about! He then removed the body to the stock shed to await further instructions. The overseer of the poorhouse wrote to the coroner to gain permission to bury the child on the Monday. That day a local woman approached Thackery, telling him of her suspicions of who the mother was. Harrard was taken by the beadle and the overseer to the stock house, where the body of her child lay under a cloth. She refused to look at the baby boy, saying, 'Oh tis my child, born of my body', and when asked how she knew it was her child she said, 'it was, and I am sorry for what I have done by it'. Harrard was deemed too ill to travel under arrest to Newgate Prison so spent the next two days under the watchful eye of a midwife.

On Thursday night Harrard asked about John Gadd, who had gone to (Market) Drayton to bring in wheat. Perhaps she was working out a way of getting rid of her lover and also her tormenter who regularly beat her when he was drunk. Later she tried to say that Gadd had taken the baby from her and she had never heard of it again until the stock house. At her trial it was revealed that Harrard was examined by a midwife and asked if she had given birth, to which she replied, 'yes, as I stepped over a stile it started to come but men were approaching so I quickly went towards the river when it came out'. 'Was it alive?' asked the Midwife. 'No.' The midwife stated that the signs of bruising and the congealed blood at the point of the head wound prove the boy was alive at birth and for at least an hour afterwards. The boy was dead by the time he was thrown into the river. When asked if she, Harrard, had made provision for the birth of the child, she said that she had been given two bonnets but had given them away. This was a further black mark against her as many a woman accused of infanticide had won their freedom by showing they had clothing and goods for the child they had hoped would live. Under further questioning at the trial Harrard claimed that she had gone to Richmond to seek work but had fallen ill and needed to sit down for two hours but was moved on by the beadle there, despite her request for help. She then went to Twickenham, where she again tried to gain help but was turned away to fields nearby after being called a bitch. It was in that field, after crossing the stile, that she gave birth near the river. John Gadd was called and stated that he was aware that some months before Harrard had suffered a miscarriage but seemed unaware that she was pregnant this time. She wept as he left the room and was not to see him again for soon after the jury were dismissed to give their verdict – guilty. She was executed for infanticide on 6 September 1739 and buried in the graveyard at Newgate Prison.

 Another child killer was himself a child. Alfred Fitz was aged nine and lived in a slum in Liverpool. One day he lost his temper with his friend, James Fleeson, and hit him with a brick. Realising that James was dead, he went with another boy to throw the body into the Liverpool Canal. They were witnessed in the act and were subsequently caught and found guilty of manslaughter in August 1855. The death sentence was commuted to twelve months' imprisonment, which they served in Liverpool.

 Due to the murky waters of canals, they have been utilised by many a murderer, such as Joseph Hirst, aged twenty-six, who was a bricklayer, and his sweetheart Martha Goddard, twenty, a laundress. They had lived in various parts of the country before they settled in Manchester. Soon after, Martha gave birth to a baby girl. In March 1896 they moved to new lodgings in the same district. On 2 April they left the house carrying a child, telling the landlady they were taking her to Stockport to be cared for by Hirst's mother. Hirst and Goddard returned later without the child and soon afterwards a body was found floating in a nearby canal. Acting on information received, the police called on the couple and after satisfying themselves that it was their child in the canal, they charged them with murder. There were angry protests outside the Manchester Assizes on 14 July 1896, where Goddard was charged as an accessory and discharged. Hirst confessed to strangling the child after he had become tired of it crying all night. He was hanged in Manchester in August 1896, by James Billington.

For some unknown reason a labourer employed by Swansea Corporation, Thomas Nash, took his six-year-old daughter for a walk along Swansea pier. After they had chatted for a while he threw her into the sea, where she drowned. In his condemned cell he was visited by his other daughter, but his wife, so upset by what he had done, refused to see him. He was hanged on 1 March 1886 at Cardiff by James Berry.

On rare occasions a stranger can take the life of a child, as happened on 12 October 1908. Ten-year-old Eliza Warburton was one of a number of children playing in Station Road, Winsford, when they were were approached by James Phipps, a twenty-one-year-old unemployed painter. He offered two pennies as a reward to any one of them who would go and fetch some cigarettes. Eliza volunteered and when she returned with the cigarettes Phipps asked her if she knew where the local lamplighter was and she said that she would show him the way. Witnesses giving evidence at the trial said that he was seen around 7.30p.m. on a footpath heading towards wasteland with Eliza. Phipps on the day in question had a white scarf tied over one eye socket. During his schooldays he had lost an eye whilst playing with friends in the playground so always wore a patch or scarf. When he was next seen he had on a different scarf. Eliza Warburton's father was getting concerned for her whereabouts by 8p.m. so went off to search for his daughter. After knocking on a few neighbours' doors he told them he was worried about her not returning and some of them joined him in the search for Eliza. As they walked down the footpath in the direction Eliza was last seen, Phipps suddenly appeared from a hedge, saw the crowd and turned on his heels and ran off, causing Eliza's father and others to give chase. Phipps was caught and arrested by the police and held on suspicion of murder. Later that evening he confessed that he'd been teased about his missing eye and the children had thrown stones at him so he chased them, catching up with a girl who he then drowned in a shallow pool in a fit of madness. A second search using torchlight took place. Eliza's body was found face down in a pool of muddy water as described by Phipps. There were marks of the struggle and signs of a sexual assault. At his trial, through his defence solicitor, he pleaded not guilty through insanity. The jury took just seven minutes to find him guilty of murder. Exactly one month after the murder he was hanged by Henry and Thomas Pierrepoint on 12 November 1908 in Knutsford, Cheshire.

Sometimes the child of warring parents can become the victim, as little Ann was to find to her cost. Her mother, Ann Wycherly, twenty-eight, and her two illegitimate children, in December 1837, were living in the workhouse at Market Drayton, Shropshire. The older child, also named Ann, was not treated at all well by her mother, who seemed to favour the younger child she had conceived with her then lover, Charles Gilbert. On Thursday 14 December Ann left the workhouse with the two children and was seen by James Freeman in the afternoon, still with both children. By six o'clock she was exhausted and knocked on the door of a cottage where she asked if she could have some water before moving on. At that point, the owner of the cottage later stated in court, she only had the infant child with her.

On 22 December, William Poole saw something floating in a pit on his employer's land near Chipnall. After rushing to inform the farmer and returning to the pit, between them they were able to pull the small object out on to the bank where they were horrified to find it was the body of a little girl. At the inquest held at the Noah public house William Crutchley, the governor of Market Drayton workhouse, identified the body as being that of three-year-old Ann Wycherley. The cause of death was recorded as drowning, but it was noted that the girl's body and head were severely bruised. An arrest warrant was issued, allowing a lawful search for Ann. She was found in service at a nearby house, where, assisted by two local constables, she was arrested. Ann was shown her daughter's body and was reluctant to look at it. Asked why she had killed the child, she told Critchley that she would not have done so but Charles Gilbert persuaded her to do it as the child was not his. In her statement she claimed that Gilbert had helped get the poor girl into the pit and then had thrown tiles and stones at her, smashing into her face and causing the child to lose consciousness. She was tried at the Assizes in Stafford on Wednesday 14 March and the case was heard by Baron Alderson, with the prosecution led by Mr Corbett.

The governor of Market Drayton, William Crutchley, gave evidence against her and told the jury how she had left his workhouse with the two children. Catherine Biffin, another girl from the workhouse, told the jury about the way Ann had treated her daughter and how she had often seen her smacking her with a belt or stick for no reason at all. Summing up, Baron Alderson said to the jury that even if someone else had instigated it, to carry out her part in the murder did in no way diminish her guilt in the crime. The jury were asked to retire but had already spoken to each other so returned a guilty verdict almost instantly. As the sentence of death was pronounced she blurted out that she was with child. Quickly a matron and doctor were called so that Ann could be examined as to whether she was pregnant or not. They came back and said that she wasn't pregnant. However, to be on the safe side, her execution was postponed. Ann was taken off to a condemned cell where she waited a further five days and was re-examined and found not to be pregnant. Throughout the time leading up to her execution she kept implicating Charles Gilbert in the killing. Ann was able to climb the steps up to the platform, where she prayed with the Revd Buckeridge. Newspaper reports say that she struggled for less than a minute and at ten o'clock her body was taken down and moved into the prison for burial in small graveyard. No charges were ever brought against Charles Gilbert.

 Sadly there have been cases of children being murdered by their step-parents. When she was executed at Mainstone on Thursday 2 April 1868, Frances Kidder made history by becoming the last woman to be publicly hanged in Britain for the murder of her stepdaughter. Frances was born in 1843 to John and Frances Turner. In 1865 she became pregnant and was due to be married to William Kidder when she gave birth to their daughter Emma before the marriage. Frances did not know that William had two children from a previous relationship. Whilst the younger was sent to live with relatives after her mother died, his older daughter Louisa, ten, came to live with Frances and William in Kent. Frances took an instant dislike to Louisa and inflicted terrible punishments upon the girl. When she first arrived she was outgoing and excitable, yet over the next two years she became a sullen girl, cowering whenever Frances was near her. The beatings and ill treatment were all carried out behind William's back – he had no idea that his wife had been so cruel as he only saw the children on Sundays due to the long hours he worked. It was only when the next-door neighbour, William Henniker, reported Frances to the police and she was charged with cruelty that he realised what was going on and so sent Louisa to live with a guardian. Unfortunately for Louisa, William was unable to keep up with the regular payments and so she had to return to live with them.

As soon as Louisa arrived Frances started beating her again but this time openly and this led to quarrels between her and William. In 1867 Frances was injured when both she and her husband were thrown from a cart when the horse bolted during a delivery of potatoes. She took time to get over this and she had received a severe blow to the head in the accident which led to violent mood swings. On 24 August 1867 she took Louisa to visit her parents along with her own daughter, Emma. On Sunday Frances told her parents that she was not feeling too well and would not go for a walk with them, preferring to stay at home with the children. Once they left she suggested to Louisa they visit the nearby fair and told her to go and get into her old clothes before they went out. As Louisa, Emma and Frances started out on foot for New Romney they came to Cobb's Bridge. It was here that Frances grabbed Louisa and forced her into a stream under the bridge, pushing her down into the dirty water until she drowned. William had arrived in the pony and cart to pick up the three just after four o'clock on Sunday as his wife returned with Emma from their walk. He noticed Louisa was missing. When they questioned Frances about Louisa she ran upstairs and was found changing into dry clothes. The clothing she had returned in was wet and muddy, yet that they could get nothing out of her regarding Louisa. William was concerned that his wife had done something silly and when a constable was called she told him that Louisa had fallen into a ditch after being frightened by a passing horse on Cobb's Bridge. The little girl's body was soon discovered under the bridge face down in the muddy waters of the stream with footprints all around her. The body was removed to the Ship Inn to await an inquest.

The inquest opened the next day and a number of witnesses were called which led to the verdict that Louisa had been murdered by her stepmother. Frances Kidder was arrested and taken into custody to appear at the Kent Assizes at Maidstone. She spent her time at Maidstone Prison on remand for the next six months. William was greatly upset and refused to visit his wife, but gossip grew surrounding his relationship with her younger sister who was called in to help look after Emma. Frances' trial started on 12 March 1868 before Mr Justice Byles and lasted all of six hours. The prosecution used the evidence of widespread abuse of Louisa and the previous threats to kill her. However, a local doctor who examined Louisa at the Ship

Inn told the court that the girl had died from drowning, possibly caused by a fall as he could find no marks of violence on the body. There were suggestions that the witness evidence had been exaggerated and that the child had indeed fallen off a bridge and died in the shallow stream. After just minutes of deliberation the jury returned a verdict of guilty of murder and Frances was sentenced to death. William did visit on two occasions and on each occasion they quarrelled about his relationship with her younger sister, which he strongly denied. In front of an audience of around 2,000 people Frances was hanged at midday, Thursday 2 April, by William Calcraft. She struggled in the noose for some three minutes, writhing in the agonies of strangulation. Her body was left hanging for an hour and taken down before burial in an unmarked grave in the prison. The following month Parliament passed a capital punishment within prisons bill which ended public hanging.

A similar murder that shocked the area happened some years later. On 9 February 1883, the head of a young girl was found on the shore of Apley pool stuffed into a sack, a discovery that brought to light one of the most horrific murders of the nineteenth century. In the small village of Kynnersley lived Polly Mayas with her father Richard, stepmother Elizabeth and three of Elizabeth's children. Elizabeth did not want Polly and she was often seen by her neighbours neglected and starving for both food and affection. Her father worked hard to keep the family fed and often Polly was in bed when he came in from work. He did not notice his daughter's decline at the hands of his new wife. Elizabeth frequently beat Polly, with the neighbours often stepping in to stop the beatings, taking Polly home with them for safety. During one beating, Polly was knocked out cold and later died from a fractured skull. In panic, Elizabeth cut up her body and tried to burn it in the range. When that did not work she put the body parts into sacks and gave them to her husband to dump as kitchen waste. The neighbours feared the worst when Polly vanished, but Elizabeth told them that she had gone to an institution in Shrewsbury where she would be taught a trade. They all believed her, even Polly's father who had taken her broken body and thrown the sacks into Apley pool on his way to work, thinking the contents of the sacks were just rubbish. She told her husband that Polly was in an institution where she would learn to be a seamstress and she would not be allowed out until she was sixteen, until which time no contact was allowed. He initially believed his new wife but was crushed when he found out he had thrown his daughter's body into the pool of the River Severn. Once the facts about Polly's murder came to light the cottage was ransacked by an angry mob and all of Elizabeth's clothes were burnt in the street and extra police officers were drafted in to stop Wellington police station from being overrun. The mob called for both Elizabeth and her husband to be lynched, such was the outrage of the local people. When the police tried to drive a horse-drawn carriage through the crowds with the couple inside, the mob nearly turned the carriage over and mounted police had to clear the way.

Because of the high level of outrage, the two were committed for trial at Stafford, where Mr Justice Stephens heard the case on 26 April 1883. Polly's father was acquitted of murder but given eighteen months' hard labour for being an accessory after the fact. Elizabeth was said to have mental problems and so was given twenty years for manslaughter, but died within six years of her imprisonment.

Most strange is how the head was first found. Two poachers out along the banks of Apley pool claimed they saw a young girl paddling in the shallows of the pool. As they approached her, their dogs started to bark at a sack floating in reeds close to where the girl was standing. Distracted by the sack, they took their eyes off her for a second to see what was exciting the dogs. Imagine their shock upon opening the sack when they saw the partly burnt head of the girl they had just seen paddling looking up at them.

When parents die suddenly, guardians do not always do as asked. In 1751, two young boys orphaned when their parents were killed after the coach they were travelling in overturned and crashed down a nearby valley – killing all on board as well as the horses. The only surviving member of the family was their uncle, brother of the boys' father. He was initially so delighted to inherit his brother's estate that he neglected the two children, leaving them to fend for themselves, which led to them living on the scraps of food he threw to them. On the reading of the will some months later, however, he was furious to learn that his brother had left everything to the children and just 5 guineas a year for life to him. In a drunken rage, he took the two boys to the bridge over the River Dee and threw them to their deaths in the waters below. One of the brothers survived long enough to tell his would-be rescuer – a local poacher – what their uncle had done before he died. The next day, when a magistrate and gang of men forced entry into the hall, they found the uncle mysteriously dead. He was sat in a chair by the massive fireplace with a glass of wine in one hand and a look of horror on his face.

There can surely be no worse crime committed than murder by a so-called friend. On 5 January 1937, ten-year-old Mona Tinsley of Newark failed to return home from school. A number of her neighbours said they had seen her talking to a man on the Retford bus, who they believed to be lorry driver Frederick Nodder – a former lodger with the Tinsleys and known to their children as Uncle Fred. Calling himself Frederick Hudson when living with the Tinsleys, they were quite unaware of his real name or that he had a police record. It was easy to identify him as he had pronounced, staring eyes, as all the witnesses who came forward had said. Hudson, who was really Frederick Nodder, admitted under interrogation that he was with the child on the bus and that she wanted to go to stay with her aunt in Sheffield. He explained that she had got off the bus at Worksop with enough money and instructions on how to reach Sheffield. Mona never arrived. Because there was no body, the judge sentenced Nodder to seven years' imprisonment for abduction. Everyone was aware that Nodder must have murdered the little girl but no matter how often they searched rivers and canals, dredged and sifted through everything they could find, there was no sign of her. However, in June, Mona's strangled body finally floated to the surface of the River Idle with the tie known to belong to Nodder around her neck. The same judge passed the death sentence on Nodder for the murder of ten-year-old Mona Tinsley, saying, 'Justice has slowly but surely overtaken you'.

In hard times, when parents' backs are to the wall, they can act out of character, as Thomas Mellor did with his two illegitimate daughters by their mother, Ada Beecroft, who, in November 1899, died in an asylum, after having been committed. Soon after Ada's death Mellor moved in with a woman named Priscilla Redshaw, but he wasn't working and neither was Priscilla. They were evicted from their lodgings on 4 May 1900. The next day, Mellor went to visit his brother Arthur to see if there was a possibility that he, Priscilla and the girls could stay with him while Mellor looked around for work. Thomas was unable to help his brother as he too was struggling and space was tight in their two-room lodgings. When asked what he would do with the children, knowing that they had been refused entry into the workhouse, Mellor was overheard to reply to his brother, 'The water is big enough to hold them and me and all'. They eventually found squalid lodgings in exchange for handyman work Mellor promised to do for the owner. Throughout the struggles it was said that Mellor doted on the two girls and only wanted the best for them. At about 9.30p.m.

on 11 May he took his daughters out, telling Priscilla he would see her tomorrow. The three were seen that evening by two women who struck up a conversation with Mellor, who said he was trying to find a home for the two girls. Mellor was spotted at an all-night restaurant alone after midnight. Walking along the Leeds and Liverpool Canal on the morning of 12 May, William Wilson was horrified to see the two girls floating in the murky waters face down. He broke down in tears, unwilling to believe that they were really children; he hoped and prayed that they were just large rag dolls. Worse still, he realised had met them the evening before when Mellor asked him for help with his two girls. Perhaps he could have saved them – that thought stayed with him for the rest of his life.

Soon afterwards Mellor was arrested as Priscilla had become concerned about the health of the girls and their whereabouts. Mellor was being vague about where he had left them. At the police station he broke down and confessed to putting the two girls in the canal, not with the intention of drowning them but with the idea of leaving them in a shallow part of the canal where, he hoped, their cries would be heard by people in the area and the girls would be offered assistance and taken into care. In the summing up at his trial for the murder of his daughters the judge highlighted the fact that if Mellor had wanted the girls in care he should have just abandoned them in the street, where a constable would have come across them and taken them to the workhouse. It took the jury a little over an hour to return a verdict of guilty and, even taking into account the kindness Mellor previously showed his daughters, the thought that he threw the girls into the canal to drown them overrode any sympathy. Mellor was convicted of murder. He was hanged at Leeds Prison on 16 August 1900 with Charles Backhouse as the first double hanging of the century.

Another man who worried about what life was going to be like for his struggling family with a new baby in the house was William Arthur Watkins, who was separated from his legal wife and who had been living since 1946 with a woman named Florence May White. They already had a three-year-old son and Florence was now heavily pregnant with their second child. During the early hours of 21 January 1951, Florence gave birth to a healthy boy at her home in Clifton Road, Birmingham. The neighbours had been excited about having a new child in the street and constantly asked Watkins if the baby had arrived. The day of the birth he told the neighbours that, yes, a young boy had been born and that both mother and son were doing well. He was reluctant to let any of them in to see the child, which prompted a phone call to the local police station as neighbours were becoming worried that they had not seen Florence or the new baby. Having received reports that the baby had recently been born at the house and after checking with local doctors, hospitals and midwives, the police soon found out the family had had no medical person attend Florence in Clifton Road. Det. Sgt Black visited them to check on the welfare of the baby. As soon as he saw the police officer Watkins panicked and blurted out that the child was dead and that it died at birth. Watkins had taken the baby from his mother, telling her he was going to give the baby a bath. He left the bedroom only to return a few minutes later to inform Florence that her son was dead. It had slipped out of his hands and fallen into the water; before he could pull it out, it had drowned and there was nothing he could do to save it. The sergeant asked to see the baby and he was shown upstairs to the bathroom, where, still floating face-down in a pillow case, was the baby. Having seen this, Black took Watkins off to the police station for further questioning. At the station Watkins persisted with his story about the death being an accident, but he couldn't offer any reasonable explanation of how the baby ended up inside a pillow case in the water.

On 21 January, Watkins was charged with murder. Later that same day he appeared before the magistrates and was granted legal aid and remanded until 31 January, then further remanded until 8 February. When the inquest was opened and after medical evidence had confirmed the child had drowned, Watkins was further remanded until 2 March. The final magistrates hearing took place on the 15th, when Florence White testified that when Watkins had returned to the bedroom alone, he had announced, 'I've done it. The baby is dead.' He had then explained that there had been a terrible accident. In the court Det. Sgt Black told the jury that Watkins had made a false statement in the police station, part of which was read out: 'We have made no arrangements. I lost my head and did not know what to do. I went to bathe it and it slipped and I dropped it into the water. I have not slept since. If I drowned the baby, I did in the panic.' This trial opened in Birmingham before Mr Justice Finnemore on 15 March 1951 and lasted two days; Watkins, who was deaf, had to have part of the evidence repeated to him. Det. Sgt Black told the court that throughout the interview Watkins had never wavered from his suggestion that it had all been a terrible accident and that he was helping his wife: 'I got the bowl of water and was bathing the baby. It slipped and I let it drop into the water.' Under cross-examination Florence admitted that during her pregnancy Watkins had been very attentive and had urged her to go to the prenatal clinic to see a doctor, but she was too ill towards the end of the pregnancy to do so. Dr James Webster, who performed the autopsy, stated there were no external marks of violence on the baby apart from a small bruise on the nose, which might have been caused by the birth itself, and confirmed that the death was due to drowning. Now it was for the jury to decide if it was an accident or whether Watkins had done it deliberately fearing he could not afford to feed the extra child. Mr Justice Finnemore said in summing up:

> If this man was washing the baby and it fell into the bath how would it have got headfirst in a pillow case? If he put the baby into the pillow slip before it went into the water, it must throw very grave doubt on to his story that he was washing the child properly at the time of the accident.

He concluded that if his story was true, and the child had fallen into the water and no steps to rescue it were taken, he had left it in the water to die. In view of this, he suggested the jury might think that, at the least, Watkins was guilty of manslaughter. This left the jury with three possible verdicts: murder, manslaughter or simply not guilty. They took two and a half hours to decide that Watkins was guilty of murder. He was sentenced to death. In the dock Watkins just looked blankly at his partner, who was crying for him and her lost son. The provisional date of execution was announced as 24 March, giving Watkins time to make an appeal. He decided not to exercise that right, preferring instead to rely on the possibility of a reprieve. The Home Secretary said that having considered the case carefully he could not find a reason to recommend His Majesty to interfere with the due course of the law. At nine o'clock on Tuesday 3 April 1951, William Arthur Watkins was hanged at Birmingham by Albert Pierrepoint, assisted by a Henry Allen.

 When his wife delivered twins into the Gouldstone family it was too much for William Gouldstone and he was driven mad. William, of Walthamstow, was a hardworking blacksmith who had taken an oath of abstinence. In August 1883 his wife gave birth to twins. Gouldstone was concerned that they now had five children to feed and trade was falling off with the advance of machine-made iron goods. After the August bank holiday he did not return to work, which was not like him. The pressure had got too much for him and his neighbours had observed that he became very depressed over the weekend. On Sunday he cracked under the worry of how he was to feed them all. He forcibly drowned his first three children in a barrel of water downstairs whilst his wife breastfed the twins. He then burst into his own bedroom where his wife was resting on the bed with the two boys. He rushed in with a blacksmith's hammer to smash each baby's head to a pulp. His wife was left screaming in the bedroom with the bodies of the twins on either side on the blood-splattered bed. Gouldstone just walked out into the street as neighbours rushed up the stairs to find out the reason for his wife's screaming. They were horrified to discover the three children crumpled on the floor in the kitchen, soaking wet and dead. His wife was in the bedroom with the remains of her twins, covered in blood. At his trial he was described as being a man who was depressed during the months before the birth of the twins, which had pushed his mental state to the point where he did not know what he was doing. However, his statement to the police upon his arrest showed that he knew exactly what he was doing and why he was doing it, therefore, it could only lead to the punishment of death, suggested the judge. However, the Home Secretary, Sir William Harcourt, insisted that Gouldstone be reprieved from the noose and that he should undergo further medical examination but be kept in prison for the remainder of his life.

Jealousy of children that ends in murder, thankfully, is rare. Certainly when four-year-old Jimmy Dawes told his mother that grandpa was drunk and tried to kill him no one believed the poor child. His grandpa, Joseph Holden, a fifty-seven-year-old factory worker, was an alcoholic. He had taken the child to a quarry where he asked Jimmy to cut his tobacco block so that he could have a smoke. As the child did this, Holden lifted a lump of stone and threw it at the child's head. It caught his head, leaving a cut to the scalp and producing a stream of blood. Jimmy let out a cry of pain and ran off to his mother. The child was a bit of a dreamer so the rest of the family thought that he was making it all up, despite the cuts on his face and arms, which they presumed he'd got in the garden. However, Jimmy's mother, Mary, had already told her father that she thought he should leave the family home because he was causing too much trouble these days. He was absolutely livid. He had worked all his life to keep the family house together and only recently turned to drink because of the pain of various injuries he had suffered through employment. He felt that the family should now be looking after him as he had seven children. Two weeks later, a drunken Holden grabbed hold of Jimmy's brother, eight-year-old John, and dragged him to a quarry where he tied him to a rock and threw him down into the dark waters that ran near his home in Nuttall Street, Bury.

The body didn't remain underwater long and was pulled out by police after being spotted floating on the surface of the quarry. At Manchester Assizes on 13 November 1900, Holden pleaded guilty to murder and sought forgiveness from his daughter and the whole family. On Tuesday 4 December 1900 at Strangeways Prison, the sentence was carried out and Joseph Holden was hanged.

A tragic accident occurred on 17 May 1900, at Sutton in the Rolling Mills Reservoir, when a mother was seen attempting to rescue her two daughters, Lily, seven, and Agnes May, three. They were her children by John Walton, a collier of Sutton Moss. The inquest at the Locomotive Inn, Sutton, opened with the first witness, Archibald Thompson, who said that on the night in question he was near Sutton Rolling Mills and heard cries from the reservoir. He went to the side and saw Mrs Walton splashing around in the water reaching for the younger child as she held the older child in her arms about half a dozen yards from the side. There were several men on the bank but they did not go to their rescue. Mr Thompson jumped in and pulled Mrs Walton by her shawl to the side, and with the aid of Edward Williams she was lifted out. He thought the older child was alive at the time she too was pulled out but could not see the younger child, Agnes May. This evidence was corroborated by Edward Williams, John Forrester and Mary Jane Thompson, who all heard the screams and ran to assist. The coroner, Mr Brighthouse, then called for Mrs Walton, who looked dazed and in poor condition, to give evidence. When asked by the coroner how she came to be in the water she said to him and the jury, 'There is no use me saying anything, I have done the deed'. To which the coroner asked, 'What do you mean Mrs Walton?' and she replied, 'I have done it'. At this point the family doctor was called to check on the condition of Mrs Walton and it was considered that her mental condition was too weak to continue at the inquest, so she was taken home to rest. He spoke to the jury just before she left and suggested they returned an open verdict of accidental death. At this point Mrs Walton asked to speak to the coroner and the medical doctor so they retired into another room. Upon returning to the room the coroner said he was adjourning the inquiry for a further month while investigations were undertaken.

At the resumed inquest on the drowning of Lily and Agnes May Walton, Mrs Walton was absent as she had been remanded in custody on a charge of causing their deaths based on on her own confession. At the inquiry held in St Helens Town Hall the jury was told the absent Mrs Walton was simply very ill when she made her startling confession to the county coroner, Mr Brighthouse, and was still unwell, so they had to make sure it was an accident and not murder. At St Helens police court Mrs Sarah Walton of 15 Sutton Moss was charged and remanded for the wilful drowning of two children, Lily and Agnes May, at Rolling Mills Reservoir on 17 May 1900. Chief Constable Wood said that he was not holding significant evidence for the case and asked for another remand in custody for the accused. Later that month, at the inquest into the drowning of the children, Mr Walton was questioned about his wife and had said that he had been married to Sarah for twenty-seven years and had had ten children with her. He said that his wife had always been a devoted mother until the incident at the reservoir, which she always said had been an accident. She had never been in trouble with the police or caused trouble and helped neighbours when and where she could. Dr Bates was called as he had known the family as their doctor for a long time. Mrs Walton, in his opinion, was an affectionate wife and mother. When asked about her temperament, given the shock and the death of the children, he was asked if it would bring on such mania as to confess to the murder of the children. Dr Bates replied that it would have given the circumstances that she herself was immersed in the cold water and that may have clouded her judgement as well as her recollection of events. He continued that the accident may well have been that: an accident. She might also have hallucinated that she murdered her children rather than tried to rescue them. The evidence from the witness points to the fact that she had screamed, that she was in the water trying to save the children and that when she made the statement she was suffering great mental distress.

After an absence of fifteen minutes the jury found that there was reasonable cause of suspicion in conjunction with the deaths of the children, yet there was not sufficient evidence to enable them to come to a definite conclusion, so they returned an open verdict. The coroner agreed with the verdict and said in his opinion there was not sufficient evidence to send the woman to trial. However, as the jury had said that there were suspicious circumstances the case was sent to the Home Office for them to decide whether further action should be taken by the police. Mrs Sarah Walton was remanded until such time as the Home Office directed the police to prosecute or not. Mr G.W. Bailey, town clerk, said they had forwarded the disposition to the solicitor at the Home Office who would announce what view he took as to whether they should prosecute or not. The reply was that, after carefully reading the depositions, he arrived at the conclusion that the charge of murder should be withdrawn on the grounds that it rested solely upon the uncorroborated statement of the woman herself at the inquest. He thought that she was under an hallucination and that her first statement that the children had in fact drowned by accident while she was trying to rescue them was the correct one. Under the circumstances, he requested that the woman, Sarah Walton, be discharged. By mid-June Mrs Walton was discharged at the police court and freed as an innocent woman. Her solicitor, Mr Riley, who had represented Sarah, said that she was being well looked after and he was glad to say that the prospect of her health being fully restored was now possible. Mrs Walton was taken out of court by her husband and relatives. By 1901 Sarah Jane Walton suffered such mental anguish by the death of the two younger children that she was admitted to the Cheshire lunatic asylum.

Sibling rivalry has occasionally led to murder. On 29 June 1860 a person broke into a house in the village of Road, Wiltshire, and took four-year-old Francis Savile Kent from his cot, cut his throat, and dumped him in an outside lavatory. The police concluded it was an inside job and proceeded to search the house for clues. In the cellar was found a half-burned, bloodstained nightdress in the boiler furnace. When the laundress reported missing one of three nightdresses normally sent for washing by the dead boy's sixteen-year-old half-sister, Constance Kent, suspicion fell on her. Constance was a difficult child and had become worse since the arrival of her half-brother. Her mother, Mary Anne, had died in 1853 when Constance was nine and for a while she had her father's full attention. However, within months he had remarried the governess of the child, Miss Pratt, which seemed to have started a real mental instability in Constance. During the case it was realised that it would have been impossible for her to have carried the very heavy boy single-handedly across the yard, open the door and thrown the body into the lavatory as she was a weak and sickly child. The case was dismissed and she was released into the care of her father Samuel. The nursemaid who was present at the time of the murder, Elizabeth Gough, was also arrested but again there was no case against her. However, in 1865 while at school Constance made a confession to a priest, the Revd Arthur Wagner, that led to her conviction. She said that she had killed the boy with her father's razor because her father had transferred his affections to the boy's mother and Constance felt unloved. There was quite an uproar about the confession, which was supposed to be private and confidential, being used in court as evidence. It was likely that this prevented Constance from being given the

Constance Kent – the privy murderer.

death sentence. She was given life imprisonment and spent twenty years in Portland and Millbank prisons, where she trained as a nurse. In 1885 she was released at the age of forty-one and was not seen again by her family. Her name has even been linked to the 1888 Jack the Ripper murders – some have suggested she used knife skills learnt in prison to commit the horrendous murders – who knows?

Some murder by drowning cases seem clear cut, as in 1882 when Mrs Pay was charged with killing eight-year-old Georgina Moore. Mrs Pay had been the lover of building worker Stephen Moore and had moved in with him when he promised to marry her. Moore had a practice in seducing, sometimes bigamously marrying and abandoning, any willing lady he met. For a while Moore, his daughter, and Mrs Pay got on very well, until Moore found another woman to replace her and ordered her out of the lodgings. At the trial, evidence was given that the child's body was found in the River Medway close to Mrs Pay's parents' home. Georgina rarely accompanied anybody outside her home but had been seen on several occasions with Mrs Pay. It also emerged that the woman had threatened Moore that if he left her she would murder his daughter. There are a number of witnesses who saw the child with a woman the day before the body was dragged from the River Medway. None of the witnesses could confirm Mrs Pay as being the woman they had seen and her parents said that she had not been to see them for months. The jury believed that Mrs Pay had no motive to murder the child and she was acquitted.

Clearly even when the police think they have the right man or woman, it may be far from the truth. A coroner's inquest in late July 1859 was held on the death of John Thompson, a child aged four, whose death appears to be a complete mystery. Esther Latham was taken into custody on suspicion of having been connected in some way with the death of the child, but the evidence did not warrant her detention and she was discharged. The deceased was exceedingly delicate and weak, the son of a police officer from Conway Street, Everton, and it appears that some time before nine o'clock on Thursday night the mother told a servant girl to go into the street and bring the child into the house. The servant, Mary Anne Gibson, aged fifteen, went into the street but could not find the boy and after a fruitless search she returned to inform Mrs Thompson. The mother, not believing the servant, rushed outside to start her own search. When she too found no sign of John she told the servant girl to go to Rose Hill police station where her husband was working. The girl, who was perceived as being a bit simple, became confused and went to Rose Hill railway station and then walked along Blackstone Street, where witnesses recounted at the inquest that she asked for directions to Sandhills railway station. Crossing a field, she met a man who frightened her, telling her there were kidnappers in the neighbourhood and that they would strip and abuse her if they caught her out alone. She ran from the man, climbed a wall and found herself on the canal bank, and upon meeting with a man named James Fox, she asked directions to Bankfield Street. She then noticed a child floating in the water and saw a canal worker, who having been called to the scene, pulled out the body with a boathook. The body was still quite warm, but the girl did not recognise the body to be that of the missing child until it was taken to Collingswood Dock station by two police officers. Under questioning the servant admitted that she had told Fox that her mother lived in Bankfield Street. This proved to be a lie as her mother lived in Hedley Street. A boy of nine years old, Charles Hill, said that he had seen a woman named Latham kidnap the child. He said that on that evening he was playing with another lad when he saw Latham lift the child into her arms and put him under her shawl. She then ran down Gordon Street with the child, who was crying. The boy ran after the woman into Great Homer Street, but she evaded him by getting into a public house. He looked for a police officer but could not see one and hurried towards home and told Mrs Thompson what had happened. Further evidence from the wife of a warehouseman residing in Conway Street, Mrs Leahy, also threw suspicion on Latham. A witness said that at 10.45p.m. the same day she had seen Latham look into Mrs Thompson's window and laugh at the agony of the bereaved mother.

Latham was a cow keeper at Back Lansdowne Place, Everton, who solemnly declared her innocence and under questioning told police how she employed her time that Thursday. The two detectives questioned her and when they checked her statement against other witnesses they felt everything to be correct. A post-mortem on the body carried out by Dr F. Ayrton found the child had drowned. Esther Latham was put before a jury and the deputy coroner said that if they believed the evidence of the death and that Latham had actually kidnapped and murdered John Thompson, then they must find her guilty and she would be sent to the Crown Court. However, if there were any doubts in their minds then they should return an open verdict. After many hours of deliberation the jury found the verdict of wilful murder against some person or persons unknown. Esther Latham was acquitted.

 Child labour was widespread and in London, as all over the country, the conditions were terrible, with death sometimes coming as a welcome relief. Esther Hibner and her family had run an embroidery business in London's Camden Town for a number of years and they relied on work carried out by orphan apprentices from the local workhouse. In January 1829, the grandmother of one of the apprentices, Frances Colpitts, visited the establishment. She was told by Mrs Hibner and her daughter, another Esther, that the child had been naughty and could not see any visitors. The old lady was frustrated not to gain access and so complained to the parish beadle, who in turn went to the house to inspect the well-being of the child and make sure everything was all right. He was so appalled at what he saw that he made sure that six little girls were taken from the business back to the workhouse. The children were found to be starving, ragged, lousy and exhausted. Frances lay in the corner seriously ill with abscesses on the lungs. At the workhouse the children were given broth and warmth. Later they made statements about their treatment at the hands of the Hibners and their staff. Despite the care, Frances died within a few days. In the statements, the children said that they had to work from 3.30a.m. to 11p.m. every day, including Sunday, and they were kept awake by almost hourly canings. They took their four hours' sleep huddled together on the bare floors in the room in which they worked with one blanket and whatever they could pull on to themselves to keep warm. They also revealed how Frances Colpitts' injuries had occurred: the younger Esther had pulled her up by her heels and dipped her head in a bucket of freezing cold water while Mrs Hibner and Anne Robinson screamed, 'Damn her, dip her in and finish her', not drowning the child but certainly causing the illness that killed her. The jury decided that Mrs Hibner was guilty of murder and so was sentenced to be hanged. Her two accomplices, her daughter and Anne Robinson, were transported.

Throughout history children have been murdered by strangers who seem to find some pleasure by inflicting pain not only on their victim, but on the parents and family left behind. The final story in this section led to the saying 'Sweet Fanny Adams', meaning nothing at all. It all started when solicitor's clerk Frederick Baker was walking during his tea break on Saturday 24 August 1867. Baker came across Fanny Adams playing with two friends near the village of Alton, Hampshire, and he gave the girls money to run races for him across the field in which he met them. After a while he gave the two other girls some money for sweets and asked Fanny to go for a walk with him. She refused, but as her friends were now out of sight he picked her up and took her into a field. What happened next appalled everyone involved in the case. The little girl was first sexually abused before being battered to death. Baker then set about butchering the body with a filleting knife and a pen knife. The bloody severed head was stuck on a hop pole with the eyes gouged out and one ear torn off. Her chest was severed at the diaphragm and the heart was scooped out and thrown towards the river. Her arms were cut and ripped off, still clutching a copper halfpenny in each hand. One foot had been ripped off and thrown across the field towards the River Wey, where her eyes were recovered as were other parts of the girl's body and some of her clothing. After he had dismembered the girl, Baker walked on and had some beer in the Swan pub, but not before he had been stopped by Fanny's mother and group of men and women looking for her. They assumed he was innocent so let him go on his way. At his office he wrote in his diary: 'Killed a little young girl. It was fine and hot.' Within an hour Fanny Adams' body was discovered, or rather the parts of the body were discovered, and the search followed tracks of blood that led towards the town. Baker's employer noticed that he had a number of bloodstains on his trousers and particularly on the cuffs of his coat and shirt. The police soon arrived at the solicitor's office and Baker was arrested and taken away. Despite saying that he was innocent, it only took one look in his diary to realise that he was the murderer of Fanny Adams. He also fitted the description the two other girls playing with Fanny had given of the man who paid them to run in the field. On 24 December 1867 he was hanged at Winchester with a crowd of 5,000 onlookers. Baker wrote to the family before his execution begging forgiveness. The saying 'Sweet Fanny Adams' is said to originate from the murder as there was so little left intact of the girl.

The horrific murder and dismemberment of 'Sweet' Fanny Adams.

5

BABY FARMING

One of the most horrific chapters of murder in the Victorian Age must be that of the baby farmers who took away from desperate, unmarried mothers their bastard children for a payment, feeding them promises of finding the child a new home with a wealthy family. It was not until a number of cases were brought to the attention of the general public and the mothers who had given their children away that there was an outcry, resulting in various acts to stop baby farming. The National Society for the Prevention of Cruelty to Children (NSPCC) was set up around the time of the most notorious cases which led to the execution of a number of women for the murder of up to 400 children each.

Rivers and canals around the country were used to dispose of bodies from the days of child sacrifice to the baby farmers. This hideous practice was much in evidence in Victorian Britain, where one 'farmer nurse', Amelia Dyer, was thought to have murdered over 400 children handed over by their struggling mothers, who as unmarried women were deemed unclean and ostracised from polite society. Amelia Dyer became the most infamous of the baby farmers, and she used the River Thames to get rid of the bodies of her child victims. Born into a comfortable family, her father Samuel Hobley was a master shoemaker and had his own shop in the village of Pyle Marsh near Bristol. She had three older brothers and an older sister with whom she would have a strained relationship throughout her adult life after the passing of her mother, Sarah, in 1848 following an attack of typhus which left her having fits and eventually

The infamous Mrs Dyer. (*Famous Crimes*)

dying as a raving maniac. Some believe that this cast a long shadow over Amelia's life.

Amelia enjoyed reading and used this skill to train as a nurse, where she learnt many of the skills she would later rely on in the reign of her killing spree. In 1861 she married a much older man, George Thomas, who seems to have supported her whilst she trained as a nurse. During her training she met a midwife who revealed to her a way to riches in the lucrative trade of baby farming. After the birth of a daughter, Ellen Thomas (who later died), and the death of her elderly husband in 1869, Amelia needed an income, so quickly set up her home as a lodging house for unmarried mothers or mothers-to-be where she offered to take the child off their hands and into those of foster or adoptive parents. Some of her clients were prostitutes or maids who had been taken against their will and left with child; the fathers wanted rid of both and were willing to pay handsomely for the service Dyer offered. At first she did keep the babies alive for a few days before they died of starvation, but she soon realised that a quick dispatch of the child would give her more money in her pocket. In 1879 a doctor Dyer herself had called in to certify deaths of a number of children reported her to the police and the recently formed NSPCC, who arrested her. At her trial they could only prove neglect so Dyer was sentenced to six months' hard labour. She had always liked to drink and take opium in moderation, but the sentence tipped her to take more opium and at one point she was in such despair that she drank two bottles of laudanum in an attempted suicide. Soon after this she went back to baby farming and carried out the murders of the two children who were to prove her downfall.

After many changes of address to avoid being caught, Dyer, her last-born daughter Mary Ann (Polly), her son-in-law Arthur Palmer and her assistant Jane 'Granny' Smith went on to procure more infants, including Doris Marmon who they took from her mother Evalina, a well-known barmaid, for a fee of £10 and a box of clothing in January 1896. Dyer introduced herself as Mrs Harding and made a quick bond with little Doris, although Evalina took more convincing that this was the right thing for her and her child. They parted company at Gloucester, from where Dyer travelled to Willesden and not Reading as she had told Evalina. Polly was waiting for her mother and quickly got to work dispatching the child by tying a piece of white binding tape twice around her neck, topped with a tight knot. Death came slowly and later, during her confession, Dyer was heard to say she liked seeing the child struggle with the white tape tied around her little neck. In April 1896 another child was taken to Mayo Road and murdered in the same way before the two small bodies were stacked on top of two house bricks into a carpet bag. At Caversham Lock on the River Thames, Dyer slipped through the hedge and threw the bag into the water near the weir. A man walking along the road above spotted her throwing in the bag, spoke to her briefly and once she was out of sight went to retrieve it. He eventually fished the bag out of the river but was not ready for what he saw: the naked bodies of two infants, Doris Marmon and Harry Simmons, one with a length of white tape about its neck, resting on two house bricks.

The alarm was raised and the police made inquiries about the children with Dyer in mind. They eventually contacted the mothers to confirm

Caversham Lock, where Amelia Dyer threw the bodies of two babies into the river.

the link with Mrs Thomas (Amelia Dyer), the name she had used when she took charge of another child, Helena Fry, days before her body was pulled from the River Thames on 30 March 1896. The brown paper she was wrapped in had the faint name and address of a Mrs Thomas and a ticket receipt from Bristol Temple Meads railway station, where Dyer had collected Helena from her mother. The net was closing in and on 3 April police raided the house where Dyer was living. The stench of rotting flesh was so overpowering some of the officers had to open windows and wait outside before they searched the house. No bodies were found but there was plenty of evidence, including bundles of infants' clothing, pawn tickets for other bundles of clothing, telegrams and letters from mothers about adoption or enquiring about their child's progress with the new family and money. The police gathered the evidence and were shocked to realise that Dyer may have been responsible for upward of 400 child and baby deaths over her years as a baby farmer. This was to make her one of the most notorious female murderers in Britain and across the world. On 4 April she, along with her daughter and her son-in-law, was charged with the murder of many infants, including Helena Fry, Doris Marmon and Harry Simmons. Whilst in Reading Jail she wrote a plea for the lives of her daughter and son-in-law. Taken from a copy of the original it reads:

Sir,

Will you kindly grant me favour of presenting this to the magistrates on Saturday 18th instant I have made this statement out, for I may not have the opportunity then I must relieve my mind I do Know and feel my days are numbered on this earth but I do think it is an awful thing drawing innocent people into trouble I do know I shall have to answer to before my Maker in Heaven for the awful crimes I have committed but as God Almighty is my judge in Heaven on earth neither my daughter Mary Anne Palmer nor her husband Alfred Earnest Palmer I do solemnly declare neither of them had anything at all to do with it, they never knew I contemplated doing such a wicked thing until it was too late. I am speaking the truth and nothing but the truth as I hope to be forgiven, I myself and I alone must stand before my Maker in Heaven to give a answer for it all witness my hand Amelia Dyer – April 16, 1896

The charge against her son-in-law was dropped but the charge of murder still stood against her daughter. On 22 May 1896 Dyer was at the Old Bailey where she pleaded guilty to the murder of Doris Marmon by damning evidence from her daughter, the man who had seen her with the carpet bag at Caversham Lock and the mounds of clothing and correspondence. The jury took just four and a half minutes to reach the verdict of guilty. Despite her defence of insanity being pleaded to the judge, he sentenced her to death by hanging. In the weeks to her execution on 10 June 1896 she filled five writing pads with her confession, containing many new names and addresses of where she had lived and killed.

Just before she went to the gallows at Newgate Prison, where her executioner John Billington waited, she heard that all charges had been dropped against her daughter, who was now a free person. Dyer was executed at 9a.m. Such was the popular revulsion of her actions that a ballad was written:

> The old baby farmer, the wretched Miss Dyer,
> At the Old Bailey her wages is paid,
> In times long ago we'd'a' made a big fire
> And roasted so nicely that wicked old jade

Another infamous baby farmer was Amelia Sach, who ran a home for unmarried mothers and would offer to find homes for the newborns in exchange for a fee of between £3 and £5. For this she would find a suitable foster home where the child would grow up in safety or at least hat is what she promised the mother. The truth was far murkier, for no sooner had

A curious gathering.
(*Famous Crimes*)

Amelia Dyer.

River Thames, near Caversham Lock.

the mother handed over the child and fee than Sach passed the infant to her accomplice, Annie Walker. Walker, who was described in the trial as not among the brightest of people, would murder the child by pressing a pad soaked in chloroform to its face that caused the child to choke to death, and should this fail she strangled the child with her bare hands. Once dead, the clothes were removed and the naked body thrown into the River Thames or buried on a rubbish heap close to the house as soon as night fell so as to escape detection. Walker eventually gave away the sordid practice when she was lodging with a serving police officer. She rented a small room and on one occasion arrived home with a newborn child she claimed was a boy. This drew suspicion as the police officer and his wife noticed the child was in fact a girl. A few days later, Walker banged on the police officer's door holding the dead girl in her arms. The child showed no signs of being injured and Walker appeared genuinely upset by the death of the child, so much so that the police officer's wife sat with her for part of that day. When Walker returned to the lodgings with a second child a few days later the police officer began to ask Walker where she was finding these children. It was not until three days later when that child had also died that Walker was arrested and taken to the police station for questioning. Eventually she confessed to the murders of countless children for her partner-in-crime, Amelia Sach, of whom the police were aware but had no evidence to prove that her establishment was doing anything improper.

The River Thames was dredged near the home and several childen's bodies were pulled out of the river, all showing signs of being strangled. The home was raided and Amelia arrested for the act of murdering an unknown number of children. Inside the house were piles of children's clothing that Sach would sell to the parting mothers so that their child could go to their new home in clean clothes. Little did they know that in the next room the child would meet its end and the clothes be removed ready for resale to the next victim's mother. At the trial, on 15 and 16 June 1903, which investigated all the gruesome facts about the two and their treatment of the mothers and children, the jury took just four minutes to find both parties guilty of deception and murder. Henry Pierrepoint, assisted by William Billington, performed the execution on 3 February 1903 and they became the first women to be hanged at the new women's Holloway Prison and the last double female hanging in Britain.

 Like Sach and Walker, Ada Chard-Williams offered to take children from unmarried mothers and to find them suitable foster homes. These opportunistic murderers took advantage of the fact that an unmarried woman at this time was seen as a social outcast, unable to get a job or ask for assistance from the state. Sending a child to a home where it would be safe and cared for meant a lot to these women, who could then seek employment child-free. Chard-Williams had the pen name of 'Mrs Hewetson' and rented a mailbox in a newspaper shop for which she paid a small weekly sum, a clever way of receiving letters from new mothers or mothers-to-be without her real address becoming known. The mother who was to bring down this web of deceit and murder was Florence Jones, who had been offered a new job in the country but there was no place for the child. She had written to Mrs Hewetson and received a reply from her suggesting a meeting in London. They met and Jones felt that Mrs Hewetson was a kindly woman who would not harm her child and could find her a home. She handed over her daughter and three of the five pounds Hewetson had requested as the fee for finding a foster home. The following week Jones returned to the flat where she had met Mrs Hewetson only to find she was long gone along with her daughter. Fearing for the child's life, she soon found a police officer who took her to the local police station where she gave a statement about Mrs Hewetson, her child and the money she had handed over. The police visited the newspaper shop and discovered that Mrs Hewetson was in fact Mrs Ada Chard-Williams, who lived some distance from the shop. On arrival at the address given they were told that Chard-Williams and her husband had left suddenly, leaving behind some belongings and unpaid rent. That week, on 27 September 1899, the body of a baby girl was washed up on the banks of the River Thames at Battersea. A distressed Florence Jones confirmed it was her daughter, who she had given over to Hewetson to be placed in a safe home.

The police released details of the murderer in the hope that someone would know where she was. They were somewhat taken aback when Chard-Williams walked into a police station and denied she had murdered the child. She claimed that the child was given over to a Mrs Smith of Croydon, yet she had no more details other than they had met at Victoria station where she had passed the baby over to Mrs Smith, who had initially contacted her about adopting a baby girl. But where was the letter? Chard-Williams then claimed that her husband had run up a bad debt, forcing them to flee, leaving behind their belongings and all the letters. What she had not realised was the police already had hold of the belongings left behind. There were a few letters to Mrs Hewetson asking how children given over to her care were, all unopened, but nothing from a Mrs Smith of Croydon. There were also bundles of children's clothes wrapped in brown greaseproof paper tied up with string and an unusual knot that was also found on the body of baby Jones and others washed up on the shores of the River Thames. Although Chard-Williams' husband had been aware of the baby farming, he had not realised the ultimate fate of the children, and he was given a term of hard labour. The crucial piece of evidence that proved Chard-Williams was guilty of the murder of Selina Jones and many other unnamed children was the unusual knot particular to her. She was found guilty of the murder of Selina Jones and hanged at Newgate Prison on 8 March 1900.

Many advertisements appeared in the large circulation papers, including the *London Times*, where, in August 1836, the following appeared:

> NURSE CHILD WANTED – OR ADOPT. The Advertiser, a widow with a small family of own, and moderate allowance from her late husband's friends, would be glad to accept the charge of a young child. Age no object. If sickly would receive a parent's care. Terms, fifteen shillings a month; or would adopt if under two months for the small sum of Twelve pounds.

On 15 February 1865, the body of a four-month-old boy was found in a ditch filled with water on the side of a road in Torquay. It was naked and wrapped only in a few pages of the *Western Times*. The mother, Mary Jane Harris, came forward to claim her son, whom she said had been staying with a baby farmer, Mrs Winsor, for 3s a week and she had last seen the baby a month before, looking well. Harris had found it hard to pay the fee so had been persuaded to allow Winsor to smother her son and dispose of him. At the trial Winsor was given a prison sentence rather than execution as there was little 'real' evidence against her. She had been very cunning in what she did and covered the deaths of the children by having a doctor visit her charges on a regular basis. Some of the babies she farmed had also found homes.

Staying in the West Country, another murderer, Annie Tooke, was a 'nurse' to the young bastard children of unmarried mothers and had taken charge of a child belonging to Mary Hopkins, from Cambourne in Cornwall, who had moved to Ide near Exeter in order to conceal her pregnancy. Hopkins' brother had persuaded her to hand the child over to Tooke. She paid a fee of £12 upfront that was to help find her son a home and 5s a week to feed and dress him. Soon afterwards, Annie left Ide and moved to Exeter early in 1879. Here she found the baby, Reginald Hyde, difficult as he grew older. By 9 May she was at breaking point and this was the last day Hyde was seen alive. On 17 May the torso of a baby missing a head, arms, legs and genitals was found in the millstream off the River Exe. Later the rest of the body was found. A butcher and doctor from Ide who knew Annie had visited her to find out how baby Reginald was. Tooke claimed that an unnamed person had taken him away a fortnight before. The police were summoned and Tooke was taken to Cambourne, where she identified Hopkins who was arrested for the murder of her son. This came as a complete shock to Hopkins, who believed her son to be alive and well. Tooke gave evidence to the chief constable of Exeter about the way the child was abducted from her care, but her story did not ring true with him, and he arrested Tooke. Under questioning Tooke broke down and confessed to smothering the child before taking the body out to the coal shed and chopping it up with the wood axe. She then, under cover of darkness, walked to the river and threw the parts in, hoping they would drift out to sea. The police examined the coal shed at her lodgings and found a number of bloodstained garments belonging to Tooke. She was tried at Exeter Court on 21 and 22 July 1879 and convicted of murder. She was executed on 11 August 1879 by William Marwood.

The Scottish baby farmer, Jessie King, lived with her partner Michael Pearson in the Cannon-mills area of Edinburgh, where she ran a small-scale baby farm. The child that was to prove her downfall was a boy named Alexander Gunn who, at the start of his stay with King, was a well turned out and happy child. When he suddenly disappeared, some of the neighbours began to ask questions as to his whereabouts.

A gruesome job for the detectives. (*Famous Crimes*)

The mill where Annie Tooke disposed of the body.

Within a week King and Pearson had moved across the city to the Stockbridge area. It was here at Cheyne Street that she ended the lives of two further children; the body of a third was never found even though King confessed to it. Two boys discovered Alexander's body; the child had been strangled. The authorities began to ask questions about Alexander, not convinced that she telling the truth when she said he was with her sister. As they began to search the house it was reported that King broke down and confessed to the murders, taking a police officer down to the cellar and revealing the body of a baby girl. King claimed that she had killed the child by giving her too much whisky to make her sleep. In February 1889 she went on trial for the murder of the two children whose bodies had been found, but not for the one whose body was still missing. She was sent to Carlton Prison to await her fate. On 11 March 1889 she was executed by James Barry and was the last woman to be hanged in Edinburgh. It was not until 1897, when the Infant Life Protection Act came into being, that local authorities had the right to seek out baby farms, make it law that all children were to be registered with the authority and ensure that any change of custody or death be notified within forty-eight hours. The Act was given more powers under the Children's Act of 1908.

In the Gilbert and Sullivan opera *HMS Pinafore* of 1878 the character Little Buttercup is mentioned as a baby farmer:

> A many years ago
> When I was young and charming
> As some of you may know
> I practised baby-farming.

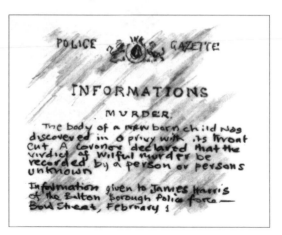

A typical police notice.

The execution of Margaret Waters.

6

RIVER DEATHS

 Murderers often find rivers, with their fast-flowing waters, convenient places for disposing of bodies. When the body of Peggy Richards was found in the Thames beside Waterloo Bridge in London on 25 June 1942, a murder inquiry began. The body showed signs of bruising on her neck, with a scarf tied tightly around it. A Canadian soldier on leave in London, Joseph McKinstry, had been seen with Richards the night before and when he turned up at the local police station with her handbag the next day he was immediately arrested. Witnesses testified that they had seen him go to the bridge with Richards and the two had exchanged money before a sexual act took place under one of the arches at Waterloo Bridge. Under questioning McKinstry denied murder but admitted the sexual act, following which he said there was a row culminating in Richards throwing her handbag at him before she ran off into the night. At his trial, which took place relatively quickly due to the war years and blackouts, the judge and the jury found him not guilty of murder.

During the blackout years in London prostitution became an epidemic in the dark streets, in turn leading to bloody and deadly turf wars that resulted in many women being found murdered in the streets of the city and in the Thames. In late 1943, the body of a naked woman was found stuffed into a sack in the River Lee near Luton, Bedfordshire. To help identify the woman her face was photographed in the morgue and displayed at every showing in cinemas in the area. There was a spate of wrong identifications. A clue found with the body, a laundry tag, led to fireman Horace 'Bertie' Manton being interviewed by the police. In December 1943 he had reported his wife missing. He said that he believed that she was having an affair with an American soldier and that she had run off with him. He had produced letters she had supposedly sent from various locations around the country but there were one or two spelling mistakes that the police quickly picked up on. During Manton's interview they asked him to take down a dictation. The same spelling mistakes appeared in his written dictation as did on the letters from his wife, which also appeared to be in his handwriting. Police searched his home expecting to find a clue that would convict Manton but all the surfaces in the house, with the exception of a pickle jar found under the stairs, were spotless so there was a suspicious lack of fingerprints. As Manton claimed his wife had lived in the house for years clearly someone had tried to remove all signs of the woman's existence. They arrested and charged Manton with murder, which led to him confessing that in the lead up to Christmas, with money being tight, they had had a massive row and at one point he had hit his wife with a stool, making her fall backwards on to a table with a terrible thud. He noticed blood trickling out of her ears, then realised that she had no pulse and was dead. In a panic he quickly undressed her and placed the body into some sacking he had from his allotment. With the blackout, he managed to get to the River Lea on his bicycle to throw her body in. At his trial the jury convicted him of murder; however, the judge announced that given his good character the sentence be commuted to life in prison. He died three years later at Parkhurst on the Isle of Wight in 1947.

Jealousy is often a factor in murder and in the case of Dr Buck Roxton, under pressure at work and suspecting that his wife was having an affair due to her constant trips away from their home and huddled conversations with their maid, his mental grip cracked. His wife Isabella was a beauty who wore elegant clothing, attracting the admiring glances of both men and women, and this had driven the her husband (a control freak by his own admission) to strangle her after he detected the odour of what he thought was aftershave when she returned home from a shopping trip. He went into their bedroom where she was changing and strangled her, but as he did so the maid, Mary Rogerson, happened to look in the room and saw him drop Isabella to the ground. A struggle ensued in which Roxton smothered Rogerson to death. He then removed both bodies to the bathroom where, with his knowledge of human anatomy, he dismembered them in the bath before wrapping them up in the local Lancashire newspaper. His plan was to

Artist's impression of Dr Buck Roxton.

drive to Scotland and dump the remains. This he did, throwing the parcels into the River Moffat. Returning home he told friends that Isabella and Mary had gone to stay with relatives. However, doubt crept into people's minds. The house was found to have blood splattered on the walls in the bathroom and Manton was seen burning clothing in the garden. He even gave away a dark, stained rug. When the body parts washed up along the banks of the Moffat the Glasgow forensic team was asked to find out who the victims were. It was the newspapers the bodies were wrapped in that led to Roxton's downfall. He confessed to the murders and was convicted, for which he was hanged at Strangeways Prison on 12 May 1936.

Another case occurred long ago along the banks of the River Greta; below Mortham Tower a terrible murder took place that rocked the small community. Margaret was the beautiful wife of Sir Thomas Rokeby, who owned Mortham Tower and ruled the area in the reign of Henry VII. He was often away on errands for the king so became suspicious when his wife withdrew her favours one night upon his return. He started to believe that she was having an affair with one of the servants and when he confronted her they had a row and Margaret ran off towards the river. Rokeby followed, as one of the male servants, who had been taking Latin lessons from Margaret, walked along the riverbank back towards the tower after throwing waste into the water. In his blind rage, Rokeby passed both his wife and the servant as he rushed towards the river. Finding no one about, he started back up towards the tower. As he headed back his wife, walking with the servant, came into view. Rokeby's anger welled up and he first sliced the servant in half with one blow from his broadsword, killing him instantly, before turning his anger on his wife, who pleaded her innocence to the end. One blow removed her head, which rolled off her shoulders to the ground. Rokeby picked up the head by its long blonde hair and hurled it into the River Greta. He returned to the tower where he stayed until his lonely death.

 A fixated and rejected admirer led to murder most foul in 1670, when local poacher William Vasey, on the orders of the estate manager, Philip Laurie, murdered the beautiful housekeeper of Beningborough Hall. Philip Laurie had, for many years, hoped the housekeeper would become his lover and was angered when he found out that the gamekeeper had called upon her and they had started to see each other. The way she met her death was terrible: she was taken from her bed, stripped, raped by the men, bound, gagged and thrown into a large sack. She was like a rat in a sack, struggling to free herself. After a short trip across the field the poacher threw the woman into the River Ouse where she was found, still bound in the sack, a little way down the river. Vasey was caught soon after breaking into a cottage, at which point he confessed to the murder that, he said, had played on his mind since he had thrown the woman into the river alive. It was only as he stood on the gallows that he told of his instructions from Laurie and the rape that had taken place led by him. Before he could be captured by an angry mob, Laurie committed suicide with his favourite shotgun.

A murder similarly motivated by rejection was carried out by Charles William Ashton, a nineteen-year-old farm labourer employed at Scrampton Farm near Malton, North Yorkshire. He was convicted of the murder of Annie Marshall, a young domestic servant employed at the same farm. On

20 September 1903, her body was found floating in a river; she had been savagely raped and then shot before being thrown into the water. Ashton confessed that he had killed her, adding that he had never intended to, but she had constantly rejected his advances and gifts. He was convicted at York Assizes before Mr Justice Grantham and recommended to mercy on account of his youth. The reprieve was refused and he was hanged in Hull by William Billington on 22 December 1903.

Not only jealousy but greed can lead to murder, as happened to Sir James Stanfield, who was the owner of Netherbow Port, where the World's End public house now stands and a number of mills near Haddington in East Lothian. Here he ran a cloth-manufacturing business successfully and with great profit. He had a son, Philip, who was the heir to the title and estate. Philip had a reputation as a thug and was often saved from serving time – and once, the noose – by his father, for which he was ever more ungrateful. He harboured a hatred for his father for being alive, thus standing in his way to the family fortune. After a bad fight with his father he was disinherited which fired his anger further. In 1687, Sir James went out for dinner with his friend and local minister, John Bell, who on occasions lodged with Sir James. Having had a hearty meal and a few drams of whisky, they retired to their bedrooms soon after reaching Sir James' home. During the night Bell was woken by loud shouting and banging in and around the house, but thought nothing of it and went back to sleep. The next morning the staff searched for Sir James who had apparently left the house in a hurry some time in the night.

Sir James' body was found in floating in the River Tyne. His estranged son Philip claimed that his father had financial worries and had committed suicide to get back at the family. When the body was recovered Philip refused to allow it into the house and insisted that the staff place it in an outhouse. The servants were then dismissed so that Philip could gather any object of worth from the house and stow it in his waiting cart. He was even seen taking the silver buckles off his father's shoes as he lay in the outhouse. As the body was found on a Sunday, Bell had already left before the body had been found as he was to give readings nearby. He was astonished when he heard the news, for at dinner Sir James had been full of ideas, pleased with the profits and enthused as to how the mills could be developed further. He and the manager of the mills were suspicious of the death and sent word to the Lord Advocate about their fears that Sir James had been murdered by his son Philip.

The body had been buried and had to be exhumed so that a post-mortem could be carried out to ascertain the cause of death. Although Philip was in attendance he was not privy to the results that were to prove his downfall. Acting as the concerned son, Philip went to hold the head of his late father as it was lowered into the coffin. As he did so, pints of blood gushed from the neck of the body all over Philip, who let out a cry to the heavens before passing out. Such was the disgust that the son of such a well-respected man could murder him in this cold calculated way that the judge Sir George Mackenzie directed the jury that God gave a signal as to the guilty one by covering him in the blood of his victim – there was no way that an innocent verdict could be option. Philip Stanfield was convicted of murder and later executed in the town, before which his tongue was cut out and burnt for lying, his right hand cut off for theft and nailed to the East Gate before his body was hung in a gibbet, bleeding to death, as a warning of what would become of anyone who might commit such a crime again.

Some people are just born bad, as was the case with John Scanlon. In 1819, Scanlon, Lord of the Manor of Barry Callaghan, near Limerick in Ireland, saw the pretty fifteen-year-old Ellie Handley one day whilst at the local market and developed lustful thoughts about her. He sent his servant to ask her to join him at the inn. Scanlon had a room there and suggested that they make love. Ellie was taken aback but also knew Scanlon was rich so demanded marriage before yielding to his desires, to which John agreed. Ellie prepared to elope with him and stole £120 savings from her guardian, who she lived with. The two were wed by an unfrocked priest who Scanlon believed had no powers to marry them, so thought the marriage was neither legal nor binding. He was shocked to hear on honeymoon that the marriage was legal and Ellie was in fact his lawful wife. He called his servant, Stephen Sullivan, to help him get rid of her now that he had had his wicked way with her and they set out to drown Ellie. They took her for a romantic row late that night, plying her with brandy before Sullivan raised the club for killing fish and struck towards Ellie's head. He missed, and as the boat rocked Ellie thought it was a bit of a joke and so started laughing merrily. Scanlon and Sullivan then clubbed her to death before stripping the body and throwing it into the river. It was washed up on 6 September 1819, just days after the happiest day of her short life. The body was quickly identified and a warrant was put out for the arrest of Scanlon, who was caught and hanged near Ballycahane, despite trying to blame his servant Sullivan. Sullivan went on the run and in early 1820 was caught and hanged for his part in the murder of Ellie Handley.

Some men find that love can turn to despair through constant nagging. Early in 1851, William Sherwood, a tailor, killed his wife and, using his shears, cut her body into pieces and scattered it throughout Norwich. He threw the pieces into the River Wensum and along tracks leading to the city. When the body parts were found, police believed they had belonged to that of a young woman. So when Sherwood announced that his wife had run off to London, aged fifty-five, they took his word for it. He was a drinker stuck in an unhappy marriage and had been driven, he later claimed at his arrest, to murder Martha because of her constant nagging and lack of capital for the business. Towards the end of 1851 a local constable visited him, looking for Mrs Sherwood. Again he told the constable that she had gone off to London and he had no idea of her whereabouts. The constable had news that would have probably saved their marriage and the business – not to mention her life – because she had been left £300 and needed to collect it in person. Sherwood had killed his wife three months before she would have inherited a fortune. Through the next eighteen years guilt, frustration and anguish built up even though he'd remarried a lovely lady and had two delightful sons. He was arrested for the murder and later

Right top: The execution of William Sherwood.

Right bottom: A grisly find: the remains of William Sherwood's wife.

that year was tried and convicted. Despite pleas for his life from his new wife and friends, he was hanged at Norwich Prison in April 1869.

 Riverside murders take place in many locations, such as the incident when a local highwayman, Thomas Wildey, was hanged for the murder of his aunt Susannah Wall and her daughter Ann Shenton on 2 May 1734. Both women kept the White Lion in Smithford Street. Wildey, a wool comber when not robbing people along the toll road, made a savage attack on his relations. His attack was a result of a bitter dispute over the pub, so in drink and armed with a cleaver and knives, he invited the two to walk with him. As they approached Ryton Bridge over the River Avon, Wildey first struck his aunt with the cleaver, rendering her incapacitated, as he turned on her daughter, whom he fancied. As her mother lay dying, she was raped before her throat was cut and her body rolled into the river. He then returned to his aunt and slashed her about the face. He did his work with such force that the body was badly cut and it took some hours to work out who she was. After the execution at the scaffold Wildey was left hanging in an iron gibbet cage at nearby Whitley Common, a grisly warning to all who passed. Some years later the cage and remains were taken down and buried in a nearby sand pit. Between 1793 and 1794 the remains were uncovered and carted away with sand to be ground down and used in the construction of the new Ryton Bridge as part of the Holyhead to London route.

 Limehouse was home to the evil vicar of Radcliffe Cross, who set up a halfway house for sailors who had hit bad times. To fund the charity he would meet rich people arriving on ships into Limehouse and befriend them before killing and robbing them. He disposed of their bodies in the River Thames from Narrow Street.

On the banks of the River Lea a police sergeant saw thirty-eight-year-old Edmund Tonbridge, a warehouseman, arguing with twenty-four-year-old Margaret Evans. Soon afterwards the police sergeant heard a splash and saw Margaret Evans' body floating past him. With help he managed to bring the woman to the riverbank and ordered that Edmund Tonbridge be arrested. Upon arrest Tonbridge claimed that they had had an argument because she had fallen pregnant by him again and wanted him to divorce his wife and marry her. When he refused, he said she took out a small bottle of cyanide from her handbag, gulped it down and staggered into the water. The police searched the riverbank and eventually found a small bottle that contained traces of poison, although the actual cause of death was never determined, despite the presence on the police force of Sir Bernard Spilsbury, who helped solve the Brides in the Bath murder case. On 18 April 1922 Edmund Hugh Tonbridge was executed by John Ellis and Robert Baxter at Pentonville Prison.

Even a glowing fiancée is not always safe from murderous intent, as was the case a mile or two to the north of Beddgelert in a place called Llam Trwsgl or 'Clumsy Leap'. Here the River Colwyn passes through a narrow cleft in the rock, 3–4ft wide, before tumbling into a deep, dark pool a distance below. This is a dangerous place for if one loses one's footing it is almost impossible to get back up the steep slopes from the deep, tumbling waters. It was at this very spot that a young man from Pennant, who had enjoyed a long engagement with a young lady from Colwyn Valley, met another girl who made such an impression that he decided to break things off with his first love. He was afraid to do so, not only because of the shame it would bring to his family, but because he feared retribution from her family because she would now be seen as a 'fallen woman'. His plan was both cruel and

The murderous vicar of Radcliffe Cross disposed of his victims in the river around Whitechapel.

Two views of the
River Colwyn at
Beddgelert.

cowardly. On the afternoon before the wedding day he went to his fiancée's house bearing presents and asked the excited bride-to-be to have a little walk with him so they could go through plans for the next day. They walked up to the jumping place over the River Colwyn. Here he convinced her that they should both jump across the gap as it would, he claimed, give them a long life and a long happy marriage. The girl was eager to do as he asked but, as he held her hand ready to jump, he suddenly threw her down into the foaming waters below and watched for a minute as, blood gushing from her gashed head, she tried to pull herself out of the water. He ran to fetch help and a huge party came from her home as many of the family had arrived the day before in preparation for the wedding the next day. Eventually the poor girl's body was pulled from the pool and her fiancé broke down in tears. Over the next few months he secretly met up with his new love and within the year they were married and had a child on the way. Although no one could prove it, the dead girl's family were convinced that this wicked man had murdered the young woman and a family feud developed.

Richard Coates was a soldier who murdered a young girl, Alice Boughen, beating her to death after his drunken attempt to rape her failed. He murdered her in a school outhouse, then carried her body down to the riverbank at Chelmsford in Essex. He intended to throw the body into the water. Although she was a slight girl he was unable to lift her body over the rails and throw it into the water as planned, so he returned to the school. It was when he was carrying the body back to the school in order to hide it that he was arrested. As a soldier he tried to blame his actions on all the horrible things he had seen whilst on duty. On 29 March 1875 he was hanged by William Marwood in Chelmsford.

Murderers frequently turn out to be the partners of the victims. One such crime was committed by Henry Dainton, a stonemason from Bath. He was convicted of the murder of his wife, who was found drowned in the River Avon on 8 September 1891. Witnesses claimed they heard a woman screaming 'Don't Harry!' shortly before the body was found. The woman was quickly identified and the police visited Henry Dainton at his home and found a bundle of saturated clothing and a pair of muddy boots. Arrested immediately, the police were lucky to get him to the station alive as an angry lynch mob had formed outside his front door. Claiming his innocence, he said that his wife had often told him that she intended to drown herself in the river. This didn't save Dainton, for on 15 December 1891 he was hanged at Shepton Mallet by James Billington.

Mothers are all too often victims of murder. James McKay was convicted of the murder of his mother, Agnes Arbuckle, after parts of her dismembered body were found in a sack on the banks of the River Clyde, while other body parts were discovered in the coal bunker of her Glasgow home. A witness in the trial told the court that McKay had invited him to Mrs Arbuckle's house on 12 October 1926 to help move the heavy tin trunk. Together they moved it to McKay's lodgings. The next day, the trunk was back at the house, but it was much lighter than when it left. Another witness said she had seen McKay on the day that his mother disappeared, covered in mud. He was sentenced by Lord Ormindale at the Glasgow Circuit Court in December 1927 and his plea of insanity was disregarded. His appeal was the first ever in a Scottish court and was heard in Edinburgh, but was dismissed when the court agreed with the original findings. He was hanged in Glasgow on 24 January 1927 by Robert Baxter.

Sometimes a father can turn into the cruel perpetrator of heinous crimes. There is a monument to one such event at the side of the A444 on the road to Bilstone from Twycross, where a gibbet post stands. Here the body of John Massey was placed in an iron gibbet after his execution for the murder of his wife and the attempted murder of his daughter in 1800. Massey was a wrestler known for his quick temper. When his wife announced she was leaving him, he lifted her in the air and tossed her into the mill-race off the River Sence. With her heavy clothing and bags she quickly sank. His daughter looked on helplessly before she too was picked up and thrown into the mill-race. She survived the attempted murder but died from pneumonia soon after her father's execution.

Legend has it that in 1630 John Graham, the miller at Lumley Mill, saw the vision of a young woman one night when he was working late. She stood a few feet away from him, her face and clothing covered in blood. Not quite believing what he was seeing and with all the courage he could muster, he asked the woman how she had received the injuries. The vision told him she was his neighbour Anne Walker, and that she had been seduced by another neighbour, John Walker, and fallen pregnant. The news of the pregnancy panicked Walker, who was not willing to take on this responsibility, and he arranged for his friend, Mark Sharp from Lancashire, to take Anne far away. Anne thought she was going to stay with an aunt to have the baby before returning to the arms of her lover. However, a short way out of the village, Sharp attacked her with a miner's pick and threw her blood-drenched body down an old water-filled pit.

Anne asked John Graham to reveal the truth about her murder. He was so terrified that he ran from the mill to his wife and stayed in bed for a week. Upon returning to work Anne visited him again, angry that he had not told the magistrates about her murder. The terrified miller again retreated home where he stayed, losing weight and becoming moodier by the day. One day his self-imposed seclusion became too much for him and he went for a walk in his garden on the eve of St Thomas. Anne appeared to him again, threatening him with her continued haunting until he revealed the truth of her murder. The next day Graham went to the magistrate to tell him the story, all the while fearing that he might be sent to an asylum or even accused of Anne's murder himself. A search was ordered around the area of the pit where, sure enough, Anne's body was found. They also found the pick, man's shoes and stockings nearby in the secret hiding place Anne had revealed to Graham. Both Sharp and Walker were arrested for her murder for which both were executed in 1631.

Love affairs can go wrong and some people seek a swift solution to their self-made problems. Thirty-six-year-old Sarah Hughes was enjoying an affair with Cadwaller Jones after he had fallen out of love with his prim and proper wife. For months they had a fiery affair until on 2 June 1877 Hughes disappeared. A week later body parts were washed up on the banks of the River Dee. After much investigation and checking through lists of missing persons over thirty years of age the authorities concluded that these were the body parts of Sarah Hughes. Over the course of the love affair the police had had cause to interview Jones and his name was put forward. Jones was arrested and soon confessed that Hughes had told him she was pregnant and began to pester him for money. After a week of her nagging he finally cracked and hit her across the head with a large stone. He then tried to disguise the body by chopping it up and throwing the parts into the river. He was hanged on 23 November 1877, aged twenty-five.

Throughout history the culprit has often been punished similarly to the way he treated his victims. Radcliffe Highway today is a busy commuter route from the City of London towards Limehouse Link, the Isles of Dogs and the River Thames. It is a far cry from what was once a notorious highway that saw murders that sent a chill down the backs of all Londoners. One dark and foggy night, 7 December 1811, just before midnight at 29 Radcliffe Highway, maid Margaret Jewell was sent by the housekeeper, Timothy Marr, to buy some oysters. Unable to find any despite a long search, she returned to find Timothy Marr, his wife, baby and their assistant dead, their throats cut. So horrific were the murders that the Government offered 500 guineas as a reward for information leading to the identity of the murderer. Just twelve days later, on 19 December, Mr Williamson, landlord of the Kings Arms public house at 81 Gravel Lane, had not long been home with his wife when a disturbance began. The upstairs lodger, John Turner, climbed out of a window shouting, 'Murder! Murder!' A crowd soon gathered and pushed in the door to found Williamson at the foot of the stairs with his throat cut, his wife and maid similarly injured and bleeding to death. An arrest was made of a sailor, John Williams, who had been a shipmate of Marr's, and who was quickly charged with all the murders. He was sent to a local prison where he took his own life before being tried. His corpse was dragged through the streets of London and the parade paused outside 29 Radcliffe Highway. The body was taken to the junction of Canon Street Road and Cable Street, where a stake was driven through his heart, his arms and legs cut from the torso, his head removed and the remains thrown into a water-filled hole. A hundred years later the body parts were rediscovered and the bones given to criminologists. The landlord of the Crown and Dolphin pub at the corner of Canon Road kept the skull as a souvenir.

 Further mysterious deaths occurred at a 220-acre farm, Lodge Barton, near Liskeard, Cornwall, where the body of Norman Wills, aged thirty-nine, was found face down in a stream on 14 December 1953. He was one of five brothers in a family that had suffered a number of suicides, including that of Norman's father. One of his brothers hanged himself and another brother shot dead his daughter then himself, and finally the oldest brother shot himself after Norman's death. Norman had been very upset the day before, after having been fined in the magistrates court for failing to keep records up to date for the farm. When his brothers found his body they only noticed footprints from Norman's boots going towards the stream. It was not until pathologist Dr F. Hocking visited the site that he spotted on the opposite bank of the stream a number of footprints, possibly up to two or three people. Lifting Norman from the stream, the brothers were very careful with his body, and they were not responsible for the injuries found later. The post-mortem revealed there was no water in the lungs, which would have suggested drowning, yet there were a number of bruises around the neck, showing signs of manual strangulation. The Home Office pathologist agreed with Dr Hocking but

The Radcliffe Highway murderer was hanged and buried in a ditch,
but his skull ended up on the bar of the Crown and Dolphin pub.

the police did not. Dr Hocking, who was convinced that it was a murder
rather than suicide, went on to speak to a fellow pathologist at Leeds
University, Professor Polston. It is still an unsolved case in Cornwall and
the death was recorded as being caused by manual strangulation and not
self-inflicted.

Another mystery began in 1938, when two salmon fishermen got a
shock as they checked their nets below Haw Bridge on the River Severn,
Gloucestershire, as they found the torso of a man. The torso was believed to
have been that of Captain William Butt who lived with his invalid wife and

her nurse. A few days before he disappeared, in January 1938, bloodstains and lumps of flesh were found on the bridge but were thought to be animal. A search for the captain was undertaken but no trace of him, other than the torso, was found. Rumours emerged of a homosexual affair with the younger Brian Sullivan whose mother was the nurse for Mrs Butt. Two weeks later Brian committed suicide by gassing himself at his home in Leckhampton, Cheltenham. Whilst searching the house for clues they found Captain Butt's car keys and bloodstained coat under flagstones in the garden.

The act of throwing bodies into rivers is rarely witnessed, but on 11 April 1875 a number of witnesses saw William McHugh and another man, William Gallagher, dragging Thomas Mooney down to a builders' yard, where McHugh threw him over the wall into the River Tees, at Barnard Castle. The victim, according to witnesses, was either drunk or had been beaten about the head. He flailed about in the water for a number of minutes before drowning as the two looked on. Because Gallagher had refused at the last minute to help McHugh throw the man into the river he was acquitted, although severely reprimanded by the judge for not preventing McHugh from committing murder. McHugh was hanged by William Marwood on 2 August 1875 in Durham.

Over the years, couples eloping to get married at Gretna Green have traditionally arrived at Skinburness seeking a ferryman who would take them across the Solway Firth. The area is remote and couples often found they had time on their hands, sometimes even days, to wait for the next ferry to land. It was on one late summer's day that an unfortunate couple stepped on to the rowboat of a ferryman and set off on what should have been a calm journey to Newbie. Sadly, however, their boat was overturned by a freak storm that raged for some minutes from the sea up the firth, towards Carlisle. All three were drowned and their bodies washed up on the shore of Moricambe Bay. There was also a bridge at one time that crossed the Solway Firth. It had a short life and was demolished between 1930 and 1932, but not before a number of people crossing from Scotland on Sunday to get a drink at English pubs were killed either by trains crossing or, after the railway closed, by falling into the water in blind drunkenness. A number of nightwatchmen tried to stop people crossing the bridge yet were often bribed with beer and spirits to allow groups over on Sundays.

Isobel Chandos was the daughter of the governor of Hereford Castle under the reign of Edward II. She fell in love with a member of the king's court staying at the castle and they quickly became lovers. However, their relationship was to be short-lived as the lover turned out to be using Isobel and her father as pawns in a plot to kill the king. When the plot was uncovered the lover was executed and, broken-hearted, Isobel travelled in a boat along the river to the site of the hanging and cursed him. By some twist of fate, Isobel was never seen alive again as her body was found pinned against a fallen tree in the river just outside Hereford. The boat, a few yards away, was found broken in two.

Fast-moving sources of water are dangerous places for even the most careful. The Old Warehouse at Ironbridge, Shropshire, is a fine example of Gothic revival architecture with its turrets and battlements. The main purpose of the building was to be a loading base for the Severn trows travelling up and down the river from and to Bristol. It is now the river museum for the Ironbridge Gorge Museum Trust. In front of the building is a slipway with tracks that were used to guide the wagons that travelled between the trows and the warehouse. During the early morning rush, when safety was but a second thought, children were used as brakemen, putting blocks under the wagons to stop them rolling too fast down the incline to the waiting trows. One young lad, who had been working through the night to get loads off a number of trows, was sleepy and did not hear the warning cry from his gangmaster. He struggled to pull his block from under the wagon he was attempting to stop. A runaway wagon, full of loaded goods, hit the lad and swept him to his death, crushing him between the wagon and the sailing barge.

During the winter months the River Severn rises and becomes treacherous, the scene of many tragedies. It was at such a time that young twins were playing on the spoil heaps of the Craven-Dunhill tile works, which consisted of waste clay and broken tiles. The recent heavy rain had made the spoil heap unstable and it collapsed as the twins played and plunged them into the river. They drowned as they were swept downriver, their bodies snared in a tree that had caught under the footbridge a few yards down. Following an exhaustive search they were spotted and their tiny bodies recovered from the river, still holding hands. They were taken to the first cottage in Ferry Road, where their distraught mother was consoled by her neighbours.

The human race has been known to carry out terrible crimes on animals, and when the bodies of two dogs were found hanging from a rope on the village bridge at Congerstone, Leicestershire, many people were sickened.

A woman driver was first on the scene, braking suddenly at the bridge after noticing a rope across the road. To her horror she found, hanging at each end of the rope, the bodies of two lurcher-type dogs. The police and RSPCA arrived and removed the dogs so the road could be re-opened to a growing line of traffic. The two animals, one a bitch of about fifteen months and the other a dog of about twelve months, were thought to have died as a result of strangulation rather than being killed before they were thrown over the bridge. This barbaric act is not the first of its kind to be discovered in the area and some fear it may even be related to satanic worship. Throughout history dogs and cats and even humans have been sacrificed by those wishing to appease the gods.

Riverbank footpaths have seen their share of crimes, as on Saturday 23 January 1909, when Latvian anarchists Paul Hefeld and Jacob Lepidus made a wage snatch at the factory gates in Chestnut Road, Tottenham. They shot the delivery driver through his leather jacket but thankfully the bullet didn't enter his body. Grabbing the wages, they shot a hole in the car's radiator to prevent it from being driven. The shots were heard at nearby Tottenham police station and the police quickly ran out into the streets. Lepidus and Hefeld ran on down the street and shot dead twelve-year-old Ralph Joscelyne as he dived behind a car. As they approached the marshes they were overtaken by PC Tyler, but he was shot at point-blank range and fell dead into the side of the marsh. The six-mile chase continued with police following on bicycles. The pair ran past the reservoir where a party of duck shooters joined in and fired rounds at the two villains, hitting them but not stopping them. At Chingford Road they hijacked a tram as police chased them up the hill in a milk float, but they shot the pony pulling the cart dead, forcing the police on foot once more. In Forest Road they abandoned the tram and stole a greengrocer's cart but made little progress until they released the handbrake which caused the cart to speed off into a ditch where one of the wheels came off, so they then ran along the bank of the River Ching. It was on a long, narrow footpath alongside the river that Hefeld jumped the fence, leaving Lepidus to fire back at the police who were now approaching him from both directions. Within yards of being caught, he turned a pistol to his head and shot himself through the eye, then fell down the bank of the river. Hefeld now raced on alone to nearby newly built cottages where he ushered a family out of the cottage at gun-point. He then ran upstairs and barricaded himself in a room. The police followed, one carrying a cutlass, the other a pistol he had borrowed from someone in the crowd. Whilst they were battering the door to try to get in, they heard a gunshot. Realising there was no way out, Hefeld used his last bullet to end his life. The money has never been recovered and it is believed that it was handed to an accomplice early on, leaving the pair as expendable decoys. The cottage at Hale was the final scene in the Tottenham tragedy.

7

UNUSUAL MURDERS
AND EVENTS

George Joseph Smith, who used the aliases Oliver George Love, John Lloyd, Charles Oliver James and Henry Williams, became known as the 'Brides in the Bath Murderer' after he was found guilty of the murders of his wives: Bessie Williams (*née* Munday) who, on 13 July 1912, was discovered drowned in the bath at 80 High Street, Herne Bay; Alice Smith (*née* Burnham) who also drowned in the bath at a Blackpool property she had rented with Smith in December 1913 – discovered by Smith upon his return from the local shops, he had a near perfect alibi; and, his last wife, Margaret Elizabeth Lloyd (*née* Lofty) who Smith 'found dead' in the bath at 14 Bismarck Road, Highgate, in December 1914; their landlady had also drowned. Smith had married seven times bigamously between 1908 and 1914 and he also had one legal marriage to Caroline Thornhill in 1898, using the alias George Love. Caroline went to prison for stealing from her employers under Smith's orders, and Smith himself was later convicted on her evidence and he was sent to prison for two years. So great were her fears of what he would do to her for this that soon after her release from prison she fled to Canada.

Smith bigamously married Florence Wilson early in 1908, yet soon moved on to his next victim, Edith Pegler, after taking all of Wilson's savings within weeks. He was to return to Pegler after every murder or bigamous marriage, always with money and tales of how well his bogus antique business was doing. All seemed to be going well and, had it not been for suspicious members of the public, Smith may well have gone on to kill many more innocent women in his quest to get rich the 'easy' way – through robbery and murder. But the landlady at the Blackpool lodgings had her suspicions about Mr Smith before and after the death of his wife Alice and asked her husband, Joseph Crossley, to write to Detective Inspector Arthur Neil about the similarities to the death of Margeret Lloyd, also found in a bath tub. The names of the husbands might be different but the photograph of Mr Lloyd resembled the Mr Smith who lost his wife in Blackpool. This letter started a manhunt that involved all the police authorities across the country and sparked the case that became known as the 'Brides in the Bath murders'. DI Neil visited the lodgings at 14 Bismarck Road and found it difficult to see how a woman could drown in such a small bath, particularly given the fact that when the body was found it was three-quarters full. This led him to interview the coroner who had carried out the autopsy and he found that although there were no indications of foul play, the coroner was uncertain how the deceased had ended up at the centre of the bath with her legs sticking out over the end.

Neither could the pathologist, Dr Bernard Spilsbury, accept that a grown person could accidently drown in any of the baths in question. Neil interviewed Dr Frank French who had examined Bessie. He recalled the concern he felt Smith had shown his wife when he took her to see the doctor twice for treatment of seizures just before she died; he believed that there was 'no reason to suspect any other cause than drowning that led to a verdict of "Death by misadventure"'. Smith seemed to develop a feeling of invincibility, every post-mortem delivering accidental death verdicts and leaving him free to collect the life insurance and estate left to him in the wills. He was thought to have been lining up another victim when Neil arrested him on 1 February 1915 in Uxbridge Road, London, for causing a false entry to be entered in a marriage register. Soon Smith admitted his aliases, which led to a very complex case for Neil and the Metropolitan Police. The key issue in the case was establishing how Smith had murdered the women without leaving marks, and it was down to Neil and Spilsbury to prove it. The bodies of the three victims, Margaret Lloyd, Bessie Williams and Alice Smith, were exhumed over the following weeks and Spilsbury carried out autopsies to find out if drowning was the cause of death. On Bessie Williams' thigh he found 'goose skin', a sign of drowning, but heard that she had been found clutching a bar of soap, which pointed to her meeting a sudden and violent end. But how had Smith done it? Both Neil and Spilsbury searched for clues in the bath tubs they had removed from the suspected murder scenes and had set up

George Joseph Smith - the 'Brides in the Bath' killer.

in the police station. They spent weeks measuring, filling the bath tubs and comparing measurements against the victims. Only when Neil hired a number of expert female deep-water divers did the breakthrough come. Having tried to push the divers of the same size as the victims under the water without the possibility of leaving a mark, they discovered they could not. Then, out of frustration, Neil pulled the feet of a diver lying in one of the half-filled bath tubs towards him. Her head went under the water before she could react. Within seconds Neil noticed that she had stopped moving. Quickly pulling her out of the bath, Neil and the doctor worked for many minutes to revive the woman, who was unconscious. All she remembered before passing out was the sudden rush of water. This was exactly what the pair needed. There was some evidence of drowning, yet not enough to cause death. The sudden flow of water into the nostrils and mouth would have been enough to induce shock, known as the 'silent killer'. Based on that evidence and the fact that Smith had moved around so often to marry so many women, three of whom were now dead, led to Smith being charged with the murder of Bessie Williams, Alice Smith and Margaret Lloyd on 23 March 1915.

At his trial, from 22 June, Smith remained silent throughout, only speaking to confirm his name as George Joseph Smith. The jury took just twenty minutes to find him guilty of murder. He was sentenced to death by Mr Justice Scrutton. He was executed at Maidstone Prison on Friday 13 July 1915, aged forty-three, by John Ellis. Charles Matthews, Director of Public Prosecutions, wrote on 1 July 1915 to the Commissioner of the Metropolitan Police concerning Divisional Detective Inspector Neil:

> I feel I ought not to allow any interval of time to pass without expressing the acknowledgement which in my opinion, the administration of justice is under to Divisional Detective Inspector Neil, and to the officers who served under him, for their untiring, able, zealous, and intelligent efforts, which played so conspicuous a part in securing the conviction which was this day obtained of the above named malefactor (Smith). [Metropolitan Police Archives]

The actor Martin Kemp starred in the television film *Brides in the Bath* in 2003, directed by Harry Bradbeer and written by Glenn Chandler.

 Another bizarre murder concerned the choice of servant for Mrs Thomas of Richmond, London. She engaged Kate (Catherine) Webster, a thirty-year-old Irish woman who had lied to get the job as a domestic servant. Webster had a string of convictions which Mrs Thomas came to hear about two months into her employment. Dissatisfied with her work, Mrs Thomas had the excuse to dismiss Webster instantly when she heard of the convictions. Webster was so enraged by this that she turned on her employer in the kitchen and pushed her head into a pot of boiling water before stabbing her to death. She then cut the body up and boiled it. She was seen by neighbours working on Sunday, generally frowned upon as it was regarded as the day of rest. The next day, Monday, Webster visited Mr and Mrs Porter of Hammersmith, some old friends she had not seen for fourteen years. They were impressed with her lovely clothing and jewellery and she told them she had married well and was now Mrs Thomas. With her she had a large, heavy bag and she asked Bobby Porter, the son of her friends, to help carry it home. As they walked over the Hammersmith Bridge Webster dropped the bag into the Thames. She then asked him to follow her back to her home. After light refreshments and, as it was getting dark, she asked if he would help her to carry a heavy trunk to Richmond Bridge. Once there they both lifted the trunk on to the parapet of the bridge and dropped it into the River Thames below. Some days later when it turned up on the shoreline of the Thames it was found to contain several body parts.

Webster was not only a thief but she was a glutton too and had been eating enormous amounts of food. A week later, after selling fresh dripping in the neighbourhood, she met a publican, John Church, who found her strangely attractive despite her being a rather plain woman. He spent three nights with her alone, which, again, caused the neighbours' curtains to twitch. On the fourth day Mr Porter and John Church were seen to be removing items from the house into a waiting removal van. The neighbours began to get suspicious as they had not seen Mrs Thomas for weeks now and they wanted to know why she was moving all her belongings out. Church and Porter innocently believed Webster to be Mrs Thomas and they called her out to deal with the neighbours' questions. When they realised that she was the servant she fled the scene of her crime and made her way to Ireland. Soon the police were all over the house and discovered boiled bones which turned out to be human and jars of dripping, evidence that Webster murdered and rendered Mrs Thomas and sold the dripping to the neighbours. She was tracked down to a house in Ireland and brought back to stand trial where she was found guilty of the murder of her employer, Mrs Thomas, and sentenced to be executed. She was hanged at Wandsworth Jail in 1879.

Sometimes higher powers may reveal impending death, as happened to a mother who lived at Edinburgh Castle, once owned by her husband, Major Griffiths. The family was often visited by their nephew, Joseph D'Arce. On one visit he had arranged to go fishing with some friends who had joined him at the castle. On the night of 6 August 1734, the night before the planned trip, Mrs Griffiths woke up screaming. She had a vision that the next day her nephew and friends would all perish when the waters would rise up around them and drag them to the bottom. Her husband tried to calm her down but she was so convinced that she woke her nephew. At breakfast she begged the rest of the party not to go out fishing but they ignored her, except Joseph, who waved them off from the shore. The day was bright with little wind and a lot of sun as the boat set off across the water, yet within an hour the wind had gathered strength and was creating huge waves. The men tried to row to shore just as the boat was engulfed by a giant wave, throwing all its passengers into the water. The only survivor was pulled to safety after treading water for many hours.

The execution of Catherine Webster for the murder of her employer.

Eric Tombe's mother had many dreams about him after he went missing in 1922; she dreamt of seeing him but wasn't sure where he was. Her son had gone missing just after the stud farm in Kent in which he was a partner burned down. His business partner, fellow ex-officer Ernest Dyer, said that he'd seen her son going off in a car just before the fire started. The insurance company refused to reimburse Dyer for fire damage because they felt that it was a fraudulent claim, perhaps even started by Tombe or Dyer. Tombe's clergyman father also found out that Dyer had forged his son's signature to give him power of attorney over the stud so that he could settle the estate and sell the land that the stud was on. In November 1922, as detectives approached the hotel room in which he was living, Dyer put a pistol to his head and shot himself before the police could capture him. Just after this incident Mrs Dyer dreamt of of her son's body, but this time he was in a well near a building she remembered being at the stud. The well was searched and the body of her son was discovered at the bottom in deep water. He had been shot once in the head and weighed down.

Those who spend time administering to the sick have sometimes been known to take lives. One such person was Dr William Palmer, a well-respected man in his home town of Rugeley, where he set up a practice having studied medicine in London. He lived in a house that backed on to the Rugeley Canal, where at least one of his victims – the pet dog – is known to have ended up. He was married to his childhood sweetheart Ann and they had five children, four of whom died before the age of five. Perhaps this was a clue to Palmer's true character.

Palmer was not impressed when his mother-in-law turned up at his new home seeking a room so that she could help her pregnant daughter. Palmer hoped the stay would be brief but the mother-in-law stayed on to see three other children born in the house. Mysteriously, the mother-in-law became ill over a short period and died with the symptoms of strychnine poisoning. Palmer's brother had died in similar circumstances. By 1855 Palmer was heavily in debt and was relying on the £14,000 from insurance taken out for his brother's death to help pay off some of his gambling debts and an ex-girlfriend who was blackmailing him. He had even taken to borrowing money from lenders linked to the underworld. Now he callously poisoned his wife Ann so that he could collect the £12,000 insurance he held against her life. Palmer had forged his mother's signature on a loan guarantee and was also worried he could face fraud charges on top of the moneylenders who were hounding him with death threats.

To get away from it all, on Tuesday 13 November 1855 Palmer went with the Rugeley postmaster and John Cook to Shrewsbury races. Cook had been articled to a solicitor, yet when he inherited £12,000 he resigned from work and spent his money on drinking and horseracing. At the races Cook won £3,000 when his horse Polestar came first in the Shrewsbury handicap race and he threw a party for all his friends. Palmer left to return to Rugeley, possibly already plotting on how to get hold of his friend's money. On Wednesday 14 November Palmer received a threatening letter from a solicitor and moneylender demanding that he pay the money back. Palmer may have considered that the only course of action was to go back to the Shrewsbury races.

That evening he dined at the Raven Inn with Cook and some of Cook's friends. Later in the evening Palmer was seen in the housekeeper's pantry by Mrs Anne Brooks from Manchester, who said she saw Palmer pouring some liquid from a small bottle into a tumbler and stirring it before putting up the gaslight to check the colour. Palmer realised she had seen him do this and appeared distressed. He then returned to the room and gave Cook the contents of the tumbler, which he swiftly drank. Within a minute he was complaining of feeling ill, saying that the drink had burned his throat. Twice a doctor was called to see Cook, who was complaining of nausea, cramps, dizziness and other symptoms of poisoning, but by Thursday 15 November he was feeling a little better and spent the rest of the day at the races, where Palmer put a lot of money on a horse and stood to win around £5,000, which would have cleared most of his debts. Unfortunately, the horse failed to win the race and Palmer was now deeply in debt. That evening Cook and Palmer returned to Rugeley where Cook stayed at the Talbot Arms hotel opposite Palmer's house. On 17 November 1855 Palmer visited Cook at the hotel and ordered him coffee. Soon afterwards Cook was taken ill and became very sick. Palmer was in and out all day visiting what people thought was his sick friend, little knowing that Palmer was probably administrating strychnine on each visit. Palmer called in on Dr Bamford, an old family friend, on 18 November because the chambermaid Elizabeth Mills had claimed that she felt sick after tasting the broth that Palmer had sent Cook. Palmer was keen to deflect suspicion from himself. On Monday 19 November he went to London with Cook's betting books, thereby managing to collect most of Cook's winnings before returning to Rugeley, where he found his friend to be slightly recovered. This was the night when the pharmacist Newton claimed Palmer bought three grains of strychnine from him at 10p.m. On Wednesday 21 November 1855, John Cook, aged just twenty-eight, died at 1a.m. Before his death Palmer was seen to administer two small pills that he claimed to be ammonia pills made up on the day because of evaporation. Soon after the pills were administered Cook sat up in bed, shrieking and throwing his arms and legs about in a fearful compulsion, then suddenly became rigid. Every muscle started to move in his body, bending him upwards, then sideways until, suddenly as it started, the movement stopped and Cook was dead. Palmer called in a neighbour to lay out the body. Later, when she gave her evidence at Palmer's trial in London, she stated that she had never seen a corpse as stiff.

Throughout his trial Palmer maintained his innocence. He claimed that all the deaths had occurred from natural causes and said that Cook was a very unfit man whose excessive drinking had only shortened his life. Palmer left his home and headed to court believing that he would be found innocent at his trial and that he would somehow pay off his debts. The jury took little time to come to the unanimous decision that Palmer was guilty of murder and so the judge passed sentence that he was to be hanged at Stafford Jail. On 14 June 1856 at 8a.m., Palmer was taken into the courtyard of Stafford Jail where he was executed by George Smith in front of an audience estimated at 50,000.

Crimes at sea can be the cruellest, as young Andrew Rose found to his cost. Captain Henry Rogers, a Scottish sailor, was in charge of the *Martha and Jane* trading ship that regularly sailed between Liverpool and Barbados. When fellow Scot Andrew Rose joined the ship, little did he know that over the next few months he was to suffer greatly at the hands of Captain Rogers and the first and second mates. No sooner had Rose got his hammock ready and returned to the deck for instructions than Rogers ordered the first mate to strike Rose across the head for being late. When Rose regained consciousness he found himself tied to the mainmast where he was severely beaten with cat-o'-nine-tails until blood trickled down his back. The rest of the crew initially tried to protect Rose but were informed that anyone who helped him would receive the same punishment. No one knew the reason for the instant dislike Captain Henry Rogers had taken to Rose. After a week of beatings Rose was a gibbering wreck and his fellow crew members advised him to jump ship, which he did at the next port of call. Unfortunately for Rose, he was captured by the first and second mate and frogmarched back to the ship where he was clapped in irons. The ship sailed for England on 11 May 1857 and for the next three weeks Rose was kept in irons except when taken out to be flogged or tortured. If he dared to speak out against the punishment, iron bolts were forced into his mouth or Rogers set his dog on to him, causing his arms and legs to be perforated with bites. Rogers even made the poor man walk naked around the deck while he, the first and second mate threw objects at his genitals. Rose was forced to eat his own excrement and was constantly lashed with cat-o'-nine-tails or bitten by the dog, resulting in blood poisoning. Maggots started to appear all over his weeping wounds. Some days Rose would be lashed to the deck in the blazing sunshine with nothing to drink and he would pray for death to bring relief.

Finally, probably getting bored, Rogers decided that he was going to hang Rose and organised a mock hanging. The next day Rose died in his sleep whilst in a barrel on a sun-baked deck. A day later the unfortunate man's body was thrown overboard and there was no mention made in the ship's log about any of the treatment he had received or the fact that he had died.

When the *Martha and Jane* docked in Liverpool the disgusted crew went straight to the police. It took a day for the police to react but soon they arrested Captain Rogers, along with his first and second mate. After further investigation all three were charged with murder and they were sentenced to death. Eventually, after some persuasion from the authorities regarding the possible decline in discipline on British merchant ships, Captain Rogers became the only one to go to the gallows, being executed on Saturday 12 September 1857 outside Kirkdale Prison. The first and second mates were transported to Australia where they lived out the rest of their lives.

8

TUNNELS AND ENGINEERED STRUCTURES

During the building of canals and waterway structures a vast number of navvies were killed through work accidents, often after heavy drinking, frequently through being blown up or drowning. One such structure was Blackwater Dam, which is 300ft (91.4m) long and 90ft (27.4m) high and built to provide hydropower to the former aluminium plant at Kinlochleven, collecting water from Black Water and Ciaran Water before draining excess into the River Leven. The flooded glen is nine miles long. It was built by 3,000 navvies between 1904 and 1909 without machines, just hard labour. The work was so hard that many a navvy died on site and was buried with concrete gravestones. They died as they worked, from exhaustion, after being blown up or from being struck in the head by the huge hammers when acting as drill or 'jumper' guides. This was the hazardous practice of holding a 5ft iron drill while it was struck by a man wielding a hammer – if it hit you there was no second chance! Some perished in snowstorms on their way back to camp from the local inns. One gravestone reads just 'George Dow, 21/3/08', whilst another, reflecting the type of people often found working these remote sites, simply reads 'Unknown'. The navvies were often loners and drifters, who found themselves outside society and working for 6*d* a day. Without them, however, we would not have these great monuments. The poem below was written following a visit to the remote site of Blackwater Dam. BBC Scotland featured the dam in the programme *The Making of Scotland* in 2010.

Blackwater reservoir.

Blackwater

These are plain graves, straightforward even though
there has been suffering here: twenty headstones,
cast one morning from the concrete for the dam
and stacked with pipes and blocks until required.
Five hundred foot of ice had already done the groundwork.
The glacier oozed and scraped, hollowed and rounded,
until only finishing touches were needed.
Three thousand men could swarm and swear,
sweat and cower and huddle from the wind.
And when the work was done
a dais was set up and crowds came out to cheer
as sluice gates clanked and water flowed.

These are plain names: William Brady,
John Day, Robert Fitch, John Wilson.
Right through that year each month
they must have buried one, and sometimes several,
each man overtaken by his personal calling
to be crushed or blown apart or drowned
and brought to this patch of grass and heather.
Some must have grumbled at the extra work,

the barked shins, the stumbling over boulders,
the thumbs stove on splintered rock.
Picks rose and fell to gouge each grave.

Yet many were lucky, escaping
with buckled limbs or jellied scars
that spoke later of their winters at the dam.
And each in the end found his own alternative,
at the Somme, or back home in Kildare
or nodding in a chair in Cumbernauld.

By David Underdown, produced with permission from the poet.
Extract from *Time Lines* published by Cinnamon Press in July 2011.

 Death was part of life for the navvies, something borne out at Blisworth Tunnel, one of the spookiest canal tunnels of the British waterways and one which has a tragic history of deaths. Before it was completed on 25 March 1805, fourteen navvies lost their lives when the section of tunnel they were working on suddenly collapsed. That year, 1796, they were struggling to get through to the other end when they hit a seam of quicksand that soon filled the tunnel. Once the bodies that could be removed were taken out for burial the rest were left in the collapsed section and the tunnel line changed to the line it is today. In 1800 a tramway was built to take goods over the hill while the tunnel was completed. The tunnel went on to claim further victims when a cargo burst into flames, causing a fireball to rage through the tunnel. Many died and several burnt bodies were recovered from blackened boats and removed to the tap room of the nearby Boat Inn.

Saddington Tunnel also saw many accidents in which a great number of men and boys died, as did Netherton where nine men perished during a roof fall and it took days to recover their bodies. The remains of at least three were left where they had been buried by the fall. At Blisworth Tunnel the canal steamer *Wasp* was being used to collect workers in the tunnel who were undertaking repairs to the tunnel roof. In the centre was a wooded channel structure, or stank, that only allowed one boat through at a time to offer a little safety to the workers. They picked up a carpenter and then made full steam ahead to the other end of the tunnel. What they did not expect was a boat being legged towards them. It had sneaked past the tunnel watchman. The crew of the steamer had just stoked up and the chimney was

Harecastle
Tunnel, where Kit
Crewbucket's body
was found.
(Kerry Dainty)

steaming thick clouds of smoke. In the haze of darkness, they saw the other boat too late and crashed into it with such speed that the boat being legged took on water straightaway and the two leggers were killed, crushed between the boats and stank. The third crew member was overcome by fumes and died holding the tiller. The crew of the steamer battled through the wreckage to reach the end of the tunnel. As they made the end they were both overcome with the fumes. One died and fell on to the door of the boiler, suffering horrific burns. The other was saved when he fell into the canal, the cold water waking him from his fume-induced stupor. He quickly jumped back on the steamer and brought her to a stop. The carpenter was also found to have died from fumes.

In 1839, a woman who worked the boats as companion and cook was murdered and her decapitated body was thrown into the waters of the Harecastle Tunnel where it was found days later. Kit (Katherine) Crewbucket was identified as the dead woman whose body was found in the water, but her head was never found.

Like water courses, old mine shafts have been deemed to be good places to dispose of murder victims, as Albert Burrows thought. He was a sixty-two-year-old married farm labourer enjoying an affair with a twenty-eight-year-old mistress named Hannah Calladine in 1918. She was born in Nantwich, Cheshire, and was the mother of a four-year-old daughter by another man. Within months she fell pregnant by Burrows and bore him a son. The problem was that Burrows was already married and had failed to tell Hannah about this until she turned up wanting to live with him at the home he shared with his wife and children in Glossop, Derbyshire. Not surprisingly his wife took exception to this and moved out. She then wanted to claim maintenance, which added to Burrows' woes. When his rent was in arrears by months and he was threatened with eviction he became desperate to find more money from somewhere – or reduce his outgoings. On 11 January 1920, he took Hannah and their son for a day out on the moors with a picnic that included some whisky. After getting Hannah and the son drunk and himself somewhat tipsy he murdered them and threw their bodies down a mineshaft which was full of water. The following day he returned with Hannah's daughter, whom he had drugged, slit her throat and threw her down the mineshaft to join her mother and half-brother. He then went back to his wife, patched things up with her and she moved back in with him, unaware of what he'd done. Over the next three years he regularly wrote to Hannah's mother, pretending that she and the children were still alive. However, when a four-year-old boy went missing in the area and it was said he had been last seen with Burrows, the police started asking questions. Burrows by now was getting old and weary and he decided to confess and take the police to the mineshaft. As the officers were lowered down they found floating in the murky black waters the body of a boy who had been sexually assaulted. Whilst they were searching one of the officers noticed clothing that was hanging on to the side of the mineshaft and, pulling it, was sickened by the sight of the skeletal remains of a child. Further investigation found the remains of one other child and the decomposing corpse of Hannah Calladine. Burrows was taken to trial at Manchester Assizes, where it took the jury just eleven minutes to find him guilty of murder. He was hanged on 8 August 1923 at Nottingham Prison by Tom Pierrepoint.

 Another man found guilty of the murder of a child born to a mistress was William Bartlett, forty-six, a Cornish miner who had an eye for the girls, but also had a wife who was about to give birth to their eighth child in as many years. Whilst his wife was pregnant he began an affair with a local district nurse and she too became pregnant by him and so, in the summer of 1882, both women gave birth. As money was tight and working in the tin mines of Cornwall was hard, Bartlett had no money to pay for the extra children. On the rare occasions he was able to be with the nurse, he said to her, 'Give me the baby – I know someone who will look after it for us and give it a good home.' The child was only two weeks old when Bartlett took it from its reluctant mother and headed off across the moors. Close to the mineshaft at Lanivet in Cornwall, Bartlett strangled the child, trussed it up in its clothing and dropped it down the mineshaft. A fellow miner who had been prospecting along some old mine shafts discovered the bundle of

144

clothing and was horrified to realise it contained a dead child. He took the child straightaway to the local magistrate and the nurse was summoned. She explained she had given the child to Bartlett who was in fact her lover and it was he who must have killed the child. Bartlett was arrested and taken to the Exeter Assizes. In the cell in which he awaited his execution his hair turned from jet black to pure white. He was hanged on Monday 13 November 1882 at Bodmin Prison. Before dying it was recorded he was a gibbering wreck and screaming for mercy for what he had done.

The Worcestershire countryside was a hard place to live in the nineteenth century. On 24 August 1829, Michael Toll became obsessed with finding his common-law wife, Annie Cook, after she left him following a violent drunken row. His search seemed fruitless until four days later when the body of a woman was found some 50ft down a coal pit, lying in water. A miner searching for coal in a disused mine came across the body. Some of Annie's injuries could not be accounted for by her fall and at the post-mortem she was found to be pregnant. Toll admitted being there after being placed near the scene by witnesses but he denied murder. He was charged, tried and the jury found him guilty of her murder. He was due to be hanged at Worcester where to the end he protested his innocence. Dying before execution, a post-mortem showed that he had swallowed several lumps of his blanket to inflame his stomach which was a common way for prisoners to bring about death before execution.

In the same county Charles Wall had taken the daughter of a woman he hoped to marry for a walk but had lost his temper with her so threw the little girl, Sally Chance, into a water-filled lime pit which caused her instant death. He was hanged at Worcester Prison.

9

SUICIDES

THE RIVER THAMES

 During the Victorian period illustrators produced endless works of women who had made suicidal leaps into the River Thames. These illustrations even made their way into shilling books that were sold in the streets and in theatres. Some illustrations were displayed in the Royal Academy of Art. Even Charles Dickens commissioned works from artists that covered drowning in the Thames. In Dickens' *Sketches of Boz*, drowning in the Thames was depicted in the etching titled 'In the River' by Hoblot Knight Brown, in which sketch a woman, Martha, looks out across the river with her toe already in the water and says, 'I know it is like me! … I know I belong to it … I know that it's the natural company of such as I am!' Dickens also described seeing 'a body washed ashore, some miles down the river, swollen disfigured mass'. Shakespeare had his character Falstaff respond to the threat of being thrown into the Thames: 'A death that I abhor; for the water swells a man; and what a thing should I had been swell'd! I should have been a mountain of mummy' (*Merry Wives of Windsor*). In most cases women seem to prefer to commit suicide by poison or drowning rather than with a gun or knife. Nancy from *Oliver Twist* also felt she was destined to drown: 'How many times,' she ponders, 'do you read of such as I who spring into the tide … it may be years hence, or it may be only months, but I shall come to that at last.' In Wapping workhouse, as taken from *The Uncommercial Traveller*, Dickens' narrator is looking down to the dirty waters from the swing bridge where he hears from a waterman 'of women always heading down here down to the water'.

During the nineteenth century women's roles were changing and they were enjoying increased mobility around the country. Poorer women became aware of their plight, able to see what they were missing, which misery drove some to suicide. Waterloo Bridge was a favourite bridge for suicides. Antonia Kavanagh claimed that Waterloo Bridge alone was worth the trip from Italy, being the finest bridge in the city. However, the river that flowed beneath it had long been the cause of a stench that percolated up through the city and was produced by the numerous streams and culverts of raw sewage that ran into Old Father Thames, as it became known. George Smeaton in the 1840s wrote:

Whoever swallows it, quaffs what is impregnated with all the filth of London and Westminster, and charged with the contents of great common sewers, with disembogue pretty in particular drudge considerable quantity of filth into the Thames; the draining from dunghills and laystalls, the refuse of hospitals, slaughterhouses, colour, lead, soap works, drug mills, gas works, the minerals and poisons used in the mechanical and manufacturing, enriched with the purifying carcasses of dogs, cats, rats and men in the mix of scouring of all the wash tops and kennels within the bills of mortality. And this is the agreeable potation extolled by the Londoners, as the finest water in world!

In 1858 the Thames smelt so foul at Westminster Bridge that the House of Commons was forced to adjourn. In the 1843 play *The Scamps of London*, the heroine drowned herself nightly, W.T. Moncreiffe capturing the daily grind of London life of the time. The melodrama *London by Night*, written by Charles Selby, was performed at the Strand Theatre in 1844 and included a woman's plummet into the Thames. George Cruikshank's *The Drunkard's Children* concludes with Emma's fall from the parapet into the river, her fatal story assembled as eight illustrations that was available for 1s at the theatre. Later, in 1872, John Devereux wrote and illustrated a book on the sites of London. He wrote:

A woman apprehended by police after a drowning attempt was driven there. Impoverished and maddened, in depths of despair having been taken from her country home by her seducer who abandon her in London and hearing her father died of a broken heart she felt there was no where else to go except to take yourself off to the river and drown. A kindly passerby was able to rush in and grabbed hold of her who saved her life. A pocket of money was

A suicidal woman dragged from the river.

got together to send her back home so she could live out her life away from London.

Thomas Hood's 1844 poem 'Bridge of Sighs' is believed to have been inspired after reading the story of Mary Fuller, a seamstress who attempted to commit suicide off the bridge. Mary, a forty-year-old single mother whose only money had been stolen, attempted to drown her children and then herself in the Regent's Canal to avoid returning to the harsh treatment of the Bethnal Green workhouse. She was condemned to death for the murder of one child, but public sympathy, anti-poor law lobbyists and demonstrations of reform led to a reduced sentence of transportation for seven years. The poem asks where were her family and loved ones, emphasising her being alone in a 'cold' and inhuman world. An excerpt from the poem reads:

The bleak wind of March
Made her tremble and shiver;
But not the dark arch,
All the black flowing river:
Mad from life's history,
Glad to deaths mystery,
Swift to be hurl'd-
Anywhere, anywhere
Out of the world!

In she plunged boldly-
No matter how coldly
The rough river ran-
Over the brink of it,
Picture it-think of it,
Dissolute Man!
Lave in it, drink of it,
Then, if you can!

In 1840, around thirty suicides were committed from this bridge, which represented 15 per cent of London's registered suicides, although these were only the suicides that were known – it is believed that, as today, this was just the tip of the iceberg as many suicides are never found. Perhaps it was the penny toll on the bridge that attracted people as it ensured privacy and therefore a greater chance of success after dropping over the parapet into the river below. *Haunted London* by Walter Thornbury, published in 1865, claimed that the bridge was a spot frequently selected by unfortunate women to meditate suicide, on account of its solitude and privacy. The famous literary painting *Ophelia* by John Everett Millais shows the female model floating in the mill pond with water lilies around her. A sinister undertone to the background of this painting was the craze for photographing Ophelia-like models in workhouses. Often, to create income to help run the asylum or to buy opium, some superintendents dressed up female inmates in costumes and placed them in baths of water surrounded by flowers to show 'authentic' photographs of the phenomenon of female suicides. The painting *Found Drowned* by George Frederick Watts portrays the body of a woman washed face up on the riverbank under an archway of Waterloo Bridge. The archway in like works of art is thought to be a symbol of the way the person died, the arch preventing a suicide entering heaven. 'Past and Present' by Augustus Egg depicts the downfall of an adulterous wife. In painting number three, *Despair*, the wife is wrapped in a shawl with the thin, small legs of her illegitimate child protruding out from it. She stares at the moon from underneath the Adelphi arches near Waterloo Bridge. The tide is out at the moment but not for long. Throughout the series of paintings she looks at her beloved moon to the end. Such is her despair that she now waits for the tide to come in and death to overtake her and her child as she stands under a poster bearing the words 'VICTIMS'. Many Victorian illustrators were fixated with death. The George Cruikshank etching shows the symbol of the arch as a woman falls from a bridge with two onlookers peering over the parapet. Her hair, dress and body are flowing in the reverse of the bridge arch as if in her unwillingness to die. As she falls to her death she covers her eyes to block out the water below and perhaps the view of the onlookers. Nevertheless, Nelly, in Sarah Whitehead's novel *Nelly Armstrong* of 1853, works as a maid in Edinburgh, becomes pregnant, loses her job and then her baby, yet despite her despair she refuses to kill herself because she hopes for a heavenly reunion with the child she lost so early on.

 In 1935, Alma Rattenbury was arrested and taken to trial for the assisted suicide of her husband. Throughout the trial, she remained calm and told the jury of her love for her husband who was dying of a long-term condition that would have seen him unable to do anything for himself. She was eventually acquitted, yet four days later, on 4 June, she took her own life at a spot known as the Three Arches Bend on the River Avon, just as the railway crosses the river. Such was her anguish that she stabbed herself six times, three times to her heart, and fell into the river where she was later found by a dog walker, washed up on a small beach.

When the naked body of Kitty Garthwaite was pulled from the River Dove at Gillamoor after she took her own life it was the start of a mini revolt for the village people. Following a brief affair with the local squire, Kitty became pregnant, much to her distress as unmarried mothers were shunned by society at the time, leading to her being thrown out of her place of work that was also her home. She pleaded with her lover to take her in, maybe even to marry her, but he told her not to darken his doorstep again before setting the dogs on her. Destitute, cut, bruised and pregnant, estranged Kitty walked to Gillamoor where she drowned herself in the river. Her clothes were neatly folded and a letter to her lover was found forgiving him for turning his back on her, which scandal caused the squire to be ostracised by the villagers.

High up on Dufton Fell is the spectacular waterfall known as the Cauldron Snout, where tragic young Isabella Addison met her end. She was the daughter of a local farmer of Brow Farm who fell in love with a miner working nearby. When he left to go to Nottingham without her, her peers regarded her as a fallen woman. She became so distraught with the pain of heartbreak and the hateful gossip she endured that some days later she threw herself off the rocks at the top of the waterfall. After two days, her battered body was found by her father below the foaming waters of the Cauldron Snout.

Poverty and the fear of the workhouse drove many people to suicide, as in April 1868, when Betty Green made her escape from the hardships of the workhouse at Gauxholme during the night as everyone slept. It was claimed she was of unsound mind, so it was no surprise the next morning when her body was found drowned in the canal close to the workhouse. The Rochdale Canal seems to have had its fair share of drowning. A little further along the canal it was reported in the *Leeds Mercury* on Wednesday 4 November 1868:

> A little before eight o'clock yesterday morning the body of an elderly man called Abraham Law was taken out of the canal at Dobroyd Pool. The deceased, who lived at Knowl, near Todmorden, must have been in the water a week. A bundle, which no doubt belonged to him, was found on the canal bank last Tuesday. This was mentioned to his relatives, but they could not believe that Law had drowned. The body was, however, brought to the surface of the water by a passing boat, and was removed to the Lord Nelson Inn to await an inquest.

James Gill may have also committed suicide in the canal. He lived at Knowlwood and had become depressed following the early death of his younger brother who had just been buried at Limeholme chapel near Todmorden in July 1870. The grave in which his brother was interned also contained his parents who had died some time earlier. His distress was clear as funeral mourners helped him get to the nearby pub where they had a funeral tea. However, James drank whisky rather than tea and by 11p.m. he was worse for drink, so his companions tried to take him home. James insisted he could get home on his own. Whether he intended to jump into the canal, whether he was attacked or whether it was an accident, no one will ever know. His body was removed from the canal near the York Hotel where it was taken to the tap room to await the arrival of the coroner. He was buried a week later with the rest of his family.

 In the churchyard of St Michael's church, Croston, Lancashire, is the memorial to little Mary Elizabeth Hudson who also escaped the cruelties of the poor house to die alone on the banks of the river aged just thirteen in 1890. Initially her body was buried in a corner of the churchyard. After some months money was raised to place her in a marked grave topped by a stone cross.

10

FILM AND TV
LOCATIONS

In the many series of *Midsomer Murders* there are several deaths that involve water. The first of these is in *Dead in the Water*, first shown in October 2004, where a body is found in the River Thames during the annual midsummer regatta. The character Guy Sweetman appears to have been killed. He had fought with his friends, but as Barnaby and Scott dig into the luxury lifestyles of members of the club, they discover a tangled network of sex, jealousy, and money problems. The location is along the River Thames, mainly Beaconsfield but also Dorchester, Oxfordshire. *Second Sight*, first shown during January 2005, starts when John Ransome is found dead in Midsomer Mere, his head covered with scorch marks. All the villagers seem to have the ability to predict future events. Was his death a result of his brother Max's research into second sight, or was it caused in a pub brawl he had with his brother-in-law Ben Kirby over a baptism? Or is he just a casualty of some strange psychic experiment? Barnaby thinks that there's more to it and starts to dig deep into the village history. The location used for this episode was Cookham, Berkshire. *The Green Man*, shown in November 2003, sees Troy win promotion to inspector but before he can decide what to do a local canal tunnel collapses while undergoing restoration. Some ancient human bones are discovered with a recent skeleton hidden amongst them. As they investigate a suspicious death Troy is directed into the woods in Midsomer Worthy, where a wild man, Tom, had been attacked by a group of youths. Locations for this episode were Sapperton Tunnel, Gloucestershire, and Harefield, Hertfordshire. *A Talent*

for Life, January 2003, is set in the village of Allanbridge, where Barnaby and Troy have to solve a double murder. Isobel and local Casanova Dr Duncan Goff are found bludgeoned to death at the nearby fishing river. There are several suspects for the murder, or was it suicide and murder? Locations include Adwell, Remenham, Oxfordshire and Haddenham, Buckinghamshire. *Birds of Prey*, again from January 2003, finds Julian Shepherd drowned and it is thought that he committed suicide as he had no access to his money, which was tied up in Midsomer Magna with the inventor Charles Edmonton's fuelless transport system. Or was it murder to cover up bad book keeping by Edmonton? The locations used were Bledlow, Buckinghamshire, Chalgrove and Oxfordshire. An earlier series had the episode *Death of a Hollow Man*, March 1998, where in Firmbassett village an elderly resident is found drowned after a violent attack. A local amateur dramatic production of *Amadeus* reveals a back stage of intrigue, passion and gossip and a whole new meaning of the stage term 'corpsing'. Locations include Gerrards Cross and Black Park, Buckinghamshire. *Dead Letters*, February 2006, joins the villagers of Midsomer Barton celebrating Oak Apple Week when a young single mother, Marion Slade, is found drowned in the local stream. Was it suicide? Had she been driven to it after the death eight years earlier of her daughter Bella? Another body is discovered and it appears that the festivities have stirred up a cocktail of adultery, unrequited love and revenge in the village, all centred on Bella Slade. Locations were Bledlow, Little Missenden and Westlington, Buckinghamshire.

Inspector Morse, played so well by the late John Thaw, uses the beautiful River Cherwell that runs through Oxford as one of its locations for the episode *The Wolvercote Tongue*, first shown in 1988, in which a wealthy American is discovered dead in her hotel of a heart attack, but Morse thinks it was murder. A valuable artefact of the lady's is missing and soon the body of the curator who was due to receive the artefact is found in the River Cherwell. The tour guide and a group of elderly American tourists become the suspects. *The Last Enemy*, shown in 1989, opens when a mutilated body is discovered in the Oxford Canal with the only clue being a tag that points to one of the university's colleges where a professor is missing. The reason seems to be the opening of a prestigious post at the university that has led to murder. All Morse needs to do is find the killer before he or she strikes again. Locations include Oxford city and the Oxford Canal. *The Wench is Dead*, first shown in 1998, centres around Morse being in hospital after a health scare, and needing something to occupy his mind from the doldrums of hospital life. He finds a book in the library about a murder on the Oxford Canal in 1859. With the help of a new recruit, they dust off the evidence and Morse unveils a clever plot that would have seen others going to the gallows for murder and not the three who did. The victim in the book, Joanna Franks, is based on the real murder of Christina Collins who was murdered on 17 June 1839 on the Trent and Mersey Canal and whose story is detailed in this book. The locations were Oxford and the Oxford Canal.

A Touch of Frost stars Sir David Jason as DI Jack Frost, and the rivers Calder and Aire, which form part of the Aire and Calder Navigation, are the waterways featured in this series. The January 1995 episode *Dead Male One* involves the body of a male being found floating in the canal, which leads to a tale surrounding false identity and the poisoning of members of the local football team, Denton Athletic. *One Man's Meat*, March 1999, again opens with a body in water, this time that of a homeless teenager, Jane Owens. She had been beaten up before being thrown into the river to drown. The locations used are the River Calder, Wakefield, Pontefract and Castleford. In the New Year Special 2002, *Mistaken Identity*, a body is found in a local reservoir with no identification whilst a couple are brutally murdered in their own home. Locations include the River Calder, Wakefield, Pontefract and Castleford.

Half Life is a film directed by Craig Rosenburg, 2006, with Demi Moore playing a bereaved mother whose son drowns in a canal next to their home after getting through an unlocked gate. She exiles herself to a remote location in 'Scotland' to finish her latest book. Far from escaping the tragedy, she is haunted by the ghost of her son who tries to communicate to her that she is in danger. The film locations were in fact the Regent's Canal, North Wales, and the beaches of Anglesey, including Llanddwyn Bay and Island.

Travelling Man, made by Granada Television, ran from 1984 to 1985. After his wrongful conviction and two-year sentence for theft, ex-Detective Inspector Alan Lomax, played by Leigh Lawson, returns to his narrowboat *Harmony* and sets off along the canals of the country in search of his son. Lomax has a number of adventures including solving murders, for which the police at first suspect him, and also runs up against members of the underworld. Shot on locations in London, canals in northern England and towns.

In December 2009, in the police soap that ended its run in 2010, *The Bill*, DCs Mickey Webb and Jack Banks examine a corpse pulled from the

Black Park, Buckinghamshire, as featured in *Midsomer Murders*.

Another Midsomer location, this time used in the episode *The Green Man*.

Thames. There is a serious neck injury to the body which has been in the water all night. The man is wearing designer clothing on top of which is a tatty old coat. The body turns out to be that of a solicitor, Jake Evens, who often helped out at a homeless shelter where the owner of the tatty coat, Reggie Sharp, is regularly seen by DC Webb, who is undercover investigating another murder. The River Thames was used for this episode, in various locations in east London.

The Grand Union Canal at Alperton was used in 1989 for the soap *Eastenders*, when the character Dirty Den was supposedly murdered and his body thrown into the canal. The body was never found; miraculously, in 2003 Dirty Den reappeared on the canal bank to cause yet more chaos in the East End, before he ended up dead once again, buried below the cellar floor of the Queen Vic.

Not to be outdone by its BBC counterpart, in 2003 ITV's *Coronation Street*, the longest-running soap opera on British television, screened possibly the most dramatic waterways-related stunt ever seen. It involved a car containing the Platt family, who had been kidnapped by their deranged stepfather Richard Hillman, the third husband of the character Gail Platt, somersaulting into the air and crashing into Portland Basin at the junction of Ashton and Huddersfield narrow canals. Gail's son David Platt was so traumatised by the actions of his stepfather that he tried to kill the rest of the family in the same location when they returned in 2007.

Dalziel and Pascoe is the story of a rough and ready police detective and his rather more gentle colleague who investigate various murders, including one in a location on the Wolverhampton branch of the Birmingham Canal and on the Fazeley Canal at Edgbaston. They also pulled a body from the Grand Union Canal, which prompted investigations into a series of other mysterious deaths.

Boon, which went on air between 1989 and 1992, centres itself on Nottingham. It follows a former fireman who turns private investigator to solve murders, deaths and blackmail, and uses sections of the Nottingham and Beeston Canal as well as the Trent Lane basin.

On the radio, *Down Payment on Death* by Jim Eldridge is a five-part series on BBC Radio 7. The story follows a retired MI7 hit man Arthur (Art) Gordo, who is asked to come out of retirement to undertake a hit for £200,000. A case containing £100,000 is left in his flat by Clark from MI7, who is then shot feet away from the entrance to Gordo's flat. He finds the body shot through the head and panics when he hears police sirens approaching. He quickly places the body in Clark's car and drives off. He dumps Clark's body in the Thames at Lime House and goes to a contact in the motor trade to have it resprayed and sold on ... so the story starts.

Further to the north, in the film *This is England* (2006), the Nottingham and Beeston Canal is used at the harrowing end of the film, showing the skinheads in a murderous rage. Shane Meadows' film was very well received, going on to win a BAFTA for best British film.

Many works of literature feature empty waterways locations and many have been adapted for the big and small screens. Several novelists have used the court records of criminal trials to create characters, including Daniel Defoe's *Moll Flanders* of 1722, made into a film in 1996. In Lancashire, having converted to Catholicism in order to wed a man she thought was a rich banker, Moll resorts to giving over her child to a baby farmer for £5 a year when she realises her husband is still married and a bankrupt gentleman.

In Shakespeare's *Hamlet*, the subject of many screen adaptations over the years, Ophelia famously drowns herself in a river, tortured with grief and driven mad in the aftermath of her father's death.

Moll Flanders, the character created by Daniel Defoe, used a baby farmer.

SELECT
BIBLIOGRAPHY

For this work numerous online resources, ancestry websites and local press and record offices were consulted, in addition to the following selection of publications:

D. Brandon & A. Brooke, *Blood on the Tracks*, The History Press
Robert Church, *Murder in East Anglia*, Robert Hale
Doings in London, 7th edn, London Press/Hodgson, 1840 (Extracts)
Walter Formby, *Haunted London*, Hurst & Blackett, 1865 (Extracts)
Patricia Gray, *Cornwall Murder File*, Halsgrove
Charles Hadfield, *British Canals*, Phoenix House, London
Hertfordshire Countryside magazine
IWA
Radio Times
L.T.C. Rolt, *The Inland Waterways of England*, George Allen & Unwin Ltd, 1950
Shropshire Star
Staffordshire Press
Towpath Talk
TV Times
Waterscape/British Waterways
Waterways World

Other titles published by The History Press

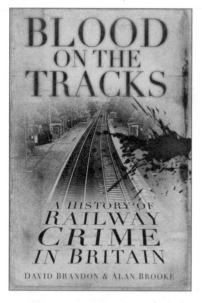

Blood on the Tracks
DAVID BRANDON & ALAN BROOKE

This fascinating history, the first of its kind, provides a murky and most intriguing account of criminal activity on Britain's railways, from its beginnings in the early nineteenth century right up to the present day. Covering all varieties of crime, from the opportunistic such as fare evasion and robberies, through the more inventive including murders, suicide on the line and railway staff 'cooking the books', to the more recent terrorist attacks, the changing nature of criminal activity on the railways can be traced through time.

987 0 7524 5231 9

Agatha Christie's True Crime Inspirations
MIKE HOLGATE

Fact proves far stranger than fiction in this collection of real-life crimes, scandals, tragedies and murders which either influenced the works of the world's most popular mystery writer or affected the lives of many famous personalities involved in her long and brilliant career.

Discover the truth behind many of her books, such as how the exploits of Jack the Ripper inspired the serial killings in The ABC Murders and how the plot twist in The Murder of Roger Ackroyd was suggested by Lord Mountbatten.

978 0 7524 5539 6

Visit our website and discover thousands of other History Press books.
www.thehistorypress.co.uk